Chinatown Lives

Asian Arts Initiative

Lisa Cancelliere

Jong Kai Chin

Wai Lum Chin

Jayson Choi

L.D.

Joseph Eng

Catharine Fan

Bihong Guan

Wai Man Ip

Benny Lai

Eric Law

Chun Moy Lee

Romana Lee

Wei Yew Lee

Harry Leong

Mitzie Mackenzie

Iwan Santoso

Khai Tang

KeKe Wang

Soo-lin Wong

Cecilia Moy Yep

Shi Xing Zeng

Chinatown Lives

Oral Histories from Philadelphia's Chinatown

Edited by Lena Sze

Photographs by Rodney Atienza

Contents

The Asian Arts Initiative's Chinatown Oral History Project, conducted from 2002-2004, has been our attempt to document the past experiences of people who lived and/or worked in Philadelphia's Chinatown while also revealing the neighborhood's complex, contemporary realities. As a community arts center with a mission of empowering Philadelphia's Asian American communities through the arts, we felt that we ourselves wanted to learn more about the Chinatown community only a few blocks away from our space. We also believed that we might be able to garner the resources to produce arts-based programming that documented and validated Chinatown as a neighborhood, something much more than a kitschy tourist draw. Through our three year effort, we produced an exhibition of photographs, a website (www.asianartsinitiative.org/oralhistory), and this book.

With the help of a mostly volunteer pool of interviewers, transcribers, and a host of community and academic contacts, we interviewed twenty-four self-identified Chinatown Philadelphians, twenty-two of whom chose to be featured in this book including one who wanted her identity concealed due to a pending refugee proceeding. In this process, we met many more people connected to Chinatown than just the ones we interviewed. The interviews were conducted by students and other volunteers, with varying degrees of oral history experience, whom we trained in a series of workshops on oral history methodology and ethics. For the most part, each interviewee (or "narrator") was interviewed between one half and two hours twice, once on a mini-disc walkman and later on digital video camera. Fourteen of the twenty-four narrators were interviewed in English and their words are reproduced, albeit in condensed form, here. Six of the narrators chose to speak in Cantonese; two in Mandarin; and two in Indonesian. For these interviews, we relied on a combination of volunteer and professional translators and interviewers and have attempted to use portions of their interviews that accurately reflect the content of the interviews as well the personality and tone of each individual narrator. Upon request by most narrators and with permission from the rest, all transcript excerpts presented here have been edited slightly from their original form to fit with standard English grammatical conventions for purposes of comprehension and continuity. This in no way implies that the English spoken by the interviewees is somehow ungrammatical or inferior to standard English. In fact, we were disappointed that we could not retain, in this monolingual book, all the richness and nuance of each narrator's voice.

In the interview, each narrator was asked about three general topic areas: personal background, relationship to Chinatown, and work/everyday life experiences. We found it important not to generalize and make assumptions about the narrator's biography, and chose to focus the interviews on these three different areas so that the interviews, as a collective body, would be somewhat structured. However, we encouraged each interviewer to be flexible in allowing the narrators to speak about other subjects. And through it all, we've learned that personal and historical events have multiple truths and perspectives.

Preface

We do not intend for this book to be the definitive publication about Philadelphia's Chinatown. *Chinatown Live(s)* does not strive for "authenticity" and is no more or less valid than any number of representations of Chinatown. We hope that we have been able to provide a portrait of this community that goes beyond the usual stereotypes but don't claim anything beyond that. This small but historically and culturally rich community is so much more than just the twenty-two stories represented here. But each of these stories is deeply moving to us in some way, because each is both emblematic and highly individualized. This book is an attempt to recapture the memories and relate the experiences of young people, adults, and elders living and/or working in this Chinatown. These portraits and interview excerpts provide a snapshot of a community, both rooted and changing.

Looking out the window of a coach bus traveling in New York's or Philadelphia's Chinatowns, we could make easy cultural assumptions about what is happening around us. Amidst the cacophony of ticket sellers, the abundance of fresh fruit and fried food stands, and the plethora of cell phone stalls that line the street, we might feel our pre-existing suspicion about Chinatown confirmed: it's a loud place characterized by recent Chinese immigrants with little education and barebones English hawking wares to unsuspecting tourists, or otherwise immersed in their inscrutable daily activities. If we do that, then we are unwittingly tapping

Essay

Lena Sze

Filled to the Brim and Finding History: Community, Storytelling, and Legacy in Chinatown, Philadelphia

deep into an orientalist vision about Chinatown, this storied "ethnic enclave." But if we make a closer examination, we might be able to discern some of the social, cultural, and economic currents running deep in this complex community.

We might sense the phenomenal changes to the social structure of Chinatown that recent Fujianese immigrants, including those who run the bus companies, have brought. As we snake through Manhattan traffic, we might get a glimpse of the poverty of recent immigrants living in tenements built in the nineteenth century or see the remnants of the old heart of Chinatown further west. We might intuit the urgency of commercial success for small

business owners or perceive the multiple layers of economic and political control that Chinatown elites exert on neighborhood residents and workers. Or we might sympathize with Chinatown's struggle to stay and grow despite commodification and gentrification.

On a good day, it only takes two hours to get from Manhattan's Chinatown to Philadelphia's. I begin this book in New York because that is where my journey, which has taken much longer than two hours, starts. I grew up in New York's Chinatown, feeling always both out of place and at home. Nevertheless, it's a sense of perceived—maybe imagined—community that keeps my parents in the same neighborhood they've been in since the 1960s and keeps me so emotionally connected to Chinatown. When I first got involved in the Asian Arts Initiative's Chinatown Oral History Project, I was motivated to learn more about this community, one state and many shades away from my own. As I spoke with more and more people, I began to feel the same familiar tug of community that I do in New York.

Immersing myself in Philadelphia's Chinatown was a project that unraveled in many stages. When I started college in the Philadelphia area, I very quickly found a tutoring and mentoring program that local college and university undergraduates conducted with school-age kids from the Chinatown neighborhood. I tutored in this program weekly for four years at the Chinese Christian Church and Center, which I only later learned was one of the keystone religious and community institutions in Philadelphia's Chinatown. When I initially came on board to work on this Oral History Project, I didn't have much context about the neighborhood and relished the opportunity to construct a deeper, truer picture of this community. Finally, this past summer I had the opportunity to live in Philadelphia's Chinatown and started to understand what it might feel like to call this Chinatown a home.

The same stereotypes and miscalculated cultural assumptions at work sitting on a bus waiting to leave one Chinatown can help us understand why Chinese immigrants founded Chinatowns in the first place. Chinatowns in the United States, including Philadelphia's, have a specific historical arc. In the mid and late 1800s, primarily Cantonese Chinese immigrated to the United States looking for fortune only to find work in difficult and easily-exploitative fields (mining, farming, railroad construction, and other types of manual labor). These immigrants, who are referred to as "sojourners," often clustered together in ethnic Chinese communities for protection against state discrimination/neglect and the threat of anti-Asian violence. Many of these Chinese immigrants later became laundry proprietors, restaurant workers, or factory workers because of continued limited employment opportunities and workforce discrimination. Because of a series of anti-Chinese immigration legislation and despite the social networks that regional or kinship associations provided, women had a limited presence in these early "bachelor communities." After World War II, immigration laws changed to allow for greater community life in established Chinatowns. In the 1960s and the decades following, immigration laws opened up even further, leading to more ethnic, language, and class diversity in Chinatowns. These are the facts that are important to all Chinatowns in the United States, but each Chinatown is more than the sum of its historical happenings and census demographics.

In many ways, Philadelphia's Chinatown has been overshadowed by the larger and older Chinatowns in San Francisco and New York. It even gets short shrift compared to equivalent communities in Boston, Seattle, and Los Angeles. But for the generations who have grown up and stayed, or grown up and left, or worked or retired here, Philadelphia's Chinatown is a community deserving its own place in the heart of the American Chinatown experience. What I found here, through these oral histories and through various

conversations, is that there are certain seminal events and recurring themes that Chinatown people share when they talk about their own identity or experience. I learned that early on Chinatown was part of the city's "red-light district," where most Philadelphians chose not to live. I learned that the surroundings, though decrepit, gave birth to generations of Chinatown youth who felt it was their home. I found out that this community is also marked by its very vocal, recent history of activism and struggle

> " It's this sense of perceived—maybe imagined—community that keeps my parents in the same neighborhood they've been in since the 1960s and keeps me so emotionally connected to Chinatown. "

against the challenge of being either boxed in or bought out of the central part of Philadelphia. In these oral histories, people share their different perspectives of the changes wrought in the last twenty or so years. I realized how much each person's perspective rested on what dialect or language they spoke, what ethnicity they were, what class they belonged to, how long they had been in the States and in Chinatown, who their families knew or didn't. I was surprised to learn about the clashes, cooperation, and suspicions between newer and older immigrants, between those who have made a conscious decision to settle here and those who have recently crossed borders and very easily enter and leave Chinatown as work or life requires.

I came to realize that this Chinatown, like the one I was raised in, is much more complex than outsiders give it credit for, much more compelling because of its contradictory stories and competing values. It's almost easier to paint a simple, romantic picture of Chinatown than a nuanced one. In these oral histories, I thought

I would only find ideas that countered mainstream representations. But I found everything, including old-fashioned or problematic narratives of hard work and immigration, a dogged belief in the "American Dream," and the challenges of biculturalism and assimilation. I came to terms with these oral histories when I stopped wanting to come to grand conclusions about them and

"But I found everything, including old-fashioned or problematic narratives of hard work and immigration, a dogged belief in the 'American Dream,' and the challenges of biculturalism and assimilation. I came to terms with these oral histories when I stopped wanting to come to grand conclusions about them and started to listen to them."

started to listen to them. These stories, after all, are not absolute truths, but shifting visions and remembrances. I've realized too these past few years that this project and its resulting book are not representative or complete. There were many people we met who we couldn't convince to share their rich histories as part of the larger story of Philadelphia's Chinatown or to see their stories as something valuable. And in the oral histories we did collect, the narrators are sometimes frustratingly silent about key points in their own lives or key aspects of Chinatown. It's also taken me a long time to realize that the story of Philadelphia's Chinatown cannot strictly be bound by its physical borders since Chinatown accumulates the memories, aspirations, and previous geographies of each person living or working in it. That's why Chinatown is filled to the brim with sometimes chafing, sometimes complementary perspectives.

Ultimately the oral history process is a humanizing one. In this book, we've tried to bring to the foreground and highlight various individuals' biographies to shed light on Philadelphia's Chinatown and larger historical and social processes. With the telling of each story, the story is relived—and becomes "live." Now that I've listened to so many stories, typed out transcripts, combed through literature and photographs, met people in meeting rooms, living rooms, bakeries, and churches, I've swallowed these oral histories, in a strange way, as part of my living legacy. I hope these stories of Philadelphia's Chinatown become part of yours.

Lena Sze
Asian Arts Initiative
2004

The history of Philadelphia's Chinatown has yet to be written. Is this surprising? Yes, considering how long people of Chinese heritage and how long ideas and things made in China have captured the imagination of Pennsylvanians—this most diverse and religiously pluralist of the original colonies. And yet, it is not surprising considering how Asian Americans have been typically cast as perpetual foreigners and newcomers—alien Americans without roots in this nation's history. Chinatowns are taken for granted. Everyone has their favorite restaurant. Tourists and city dwellers feel they know these streets, this place. So little understanding informs this surface familiarity. Chinatown is deeply embedded in popular and commercial stereotypes. Indeed, any city claiming any worldly flavor, and wanting tourist bucks, will boast of its exotic, sumptuous (all together now...) "Chi-na-town, My Chinatown." Yet what is truly known of these people and their pasts?

When would a history begin? Typically for Atlantic seaboard cities the dates cited are in the early 1870s. Quite correctly, this is when Chinese names begin appearing in directories as hand laundry operators. "Lee Fong" at 913 Race Street is cited as Philadelphia's first laundry and the beginning of the Chinese settlement. The academic research has yet to be done about this business. Was the man's last name Lee or Fong? Or were there a chain of short-term owners not named Lee or Fong who nonetheless kept the original name? Some believe these pioneers trekked east from California escaping the anti-Chinese violence that soon resulted in the 1883 Chinese Exclusion Act. Indeed, a group of Chinese California men were recruited to Captain James Hervey's North Arlington, New Jersey, steam laundry in 1870 to break the strike of Irish women. Or perhaps they migrated to Philly from the group of cutlery workers brought to Beaver Falls, Pennsylvania, from New Orleans in 1872? While all actual events and likely contributors to the early days of the Chinese Philadelphia settlement, we have to start earlier, at least a hundred years earlier, with Ben Franklin.

Along with Thomas Jefferson and Alexander Hamilton, Franklin was fascinated by the relative wealth of the Chinese empire and sought to emulate its success. Long before Wal-Mart's inexpensive Chinese-made goods, imports from China—silks, porcelains, furniture, etcetera—were eagerly sought as luxury items. Like Gucci bags and designer chocolates today, the possession and consumption of these goods conferred the social status of having good taste and arrival to genteel circles. While Hamilton sought to calculate trade advantages and Jefferson designed Chinese-like gardens, Franklin regularly noted "useful" Chinese flora, fauna, inventions, and practical folkways—such as windmills, rhubarb,

Essay   # John Kuo Wei Tchen

Here the Local Struggles Truly are Global: Philadelphia's Feisty Chinatown

silk cultivation, papermaking, and central heating—that could be adapted for a struggling new nation. He was also influenced by Chinese culture in more subtle ways. Well known for his "early to bed, early to rise" parables of work and frugality, Franklin credited a certain Chinese emperor as saying, "I will, if possible, have not Idleness in my Dominions; for if there be one man Idle, some other Man must suffer Cold and hunger." [sic] (Tchen, 17). His imagining of China and Chinese people opened up the trade and exchange interests—the pre-condition for European Americans to be open to Chinese peoples in any given locale.

The early China trade was not only about goods and ideas, it also brought the first Asians to the Atlantic seaports in the 1700s—well before the better-known movement of Chinese to San Francisco in the 1850s. In 1785 Baltimore, for example, the Pallas, a brig just returning from China, had a mix of Chinese and other Asian sailors on board. Philadelphia, I am certain, had its share of early pioneers but their lives are yet to be reconstructed in the archives. Jonathan Goldstein's study of the China trade in Philadelphia documents traders bringing Chinese servants and

> **"After helping to build the early wealth of the Pacific Coast and the China trade, Chinese were relegated to the servile work of cleaning clothing and cooking. Their individual stories cannot be understood without understanding how these 'laws as harsh as tigers' kept Chinese segregated and marginalized."**

workers to the region in these first decades of the new nation. Much more detective work in the census and other manuscripts will reveal who these people were.

The history of Philadelphia's first Asian settlement has yet to be written. (Though hopefully someone is researching this now!) Yet this book's collection of oral narratives offers us something more precious then any dry archival chronology. These twenty-two stories, in their diversity of backgrounds and time in Chinatown, illuminate a dense organic tissue of lived experiences and hard-earned insights. The paper archives rarely reveal a feeling of people struggling with external powers that limit their lives and how they've managed to survive and flourish. This feistiness embodies individuals and families making choices, charting strategies in the moment—plotting against the rock-hard limits of their situation. These retrospective stories are rejections of limiting

pasts and also leaps of faith for a better future. Collectively, they offer us glimmers of a yet to be written people's history of this community.

In these stories we begin to discover what is typical and what is unique about Philadelphia's Chinatown. What is typical, for example, are the immigration laws that framed people's lives. The stories of Wai Lum Chin, Joseph Eng, Mitzie Mackenzie, and Cecilia Moy Yep refer to "old timers" whose lives were shaped by the Chinese Exclusion Act and its legacy, effective until the opening of the immigration quotas in 1965-68. Their experiences and stories tell of three phases of Atlantic port culture Chinatowns: the early settlers who came via the China trade, then those Cantonese recruited to do the labor white men refused, and then those lives constricted by the dark days of racial exclusion. The lives of the port with ships' crews constantly flowing in and out, intermingling, forming a polyglot culture. Cecilia Moy Yep refers to the last remnants of the port culture in the bars and brothels of the 1930s. And various mission churches were originally set up to clean up the ports and convert "heathen" to proper Christian ways. Besides working on ships, Chinese laborers were recruited from California and China to provide the muscle to break through the Sierra Nevada Mountains so the Union Pacific rails could be laid. And when European immigrants took the transcontinental trains and race-mongers rejected Chinese labor, the Exclusion Law was passed and renewed. After helping to build the early wealth of the Pacific Coast and the China trade, Chinese were relegated to the servile work of cleaning clothing and cooking. Their individual stories cannot be understood without understanding how these "laws as harsh as tigers" kept Chinese segregated and marginalized.

Typical also are the generational divides that often fragment communities. Many of the interviewees came after the civil rights movement helped to repeal the racially defined immigration quotas. New immigrants from other parts of China, such as Taiwan, and other parts of Asia such as Vietnam, Indonesia, Malaysia, and other places came as immigrants to Philly's Chinatown to find a supportive environment and

"During this new era of globalization, where all local fights are also global in dimension, this community of people who have deep local and extensive global insights can guide our understanding of the future. China and Asia are no longer marginal stepchildren to U.S. interests. Rather than being 'exotic' and unusual, their experiences are becoming core to the future of this nation."

work. Others came as students and upon graduating with credentials came to Chinatown to work as professionals. Still others became part of the second- and third-generation Chinatowners while others, finding their suburban lives limited, found a community in this historic district. These post 1965 immigrants come from one set of politically charged circumstances—the 1960's Cultural Revolution in China and the U.S. war in Indochina—and enter another. Many have class advantages yet still find tough times here. Despite these tough times many find a special meaning to be working in a community setting. Youth and suburbanites have enjoyed the post-WWII prosperity of the U.S. and enjoyed much more access and rights, yet many feel rootless and seek a sense of home in these streets.

Typically, these differences of generations, dialects, languages, and cultures divide people into factions and these factions limit the ability of a place like Chinatown to fight ongoing exclusion and marginalization. New York's Chinatown is certainly divided in these ways and many more. Despite a much larger population New York's Chinatown has remained politically impotent. In this respect Philadelphia's Chinatown is not typical. Somehow the residents and workers of Chinatown have come together across traditional and class divides and successfully fought City Hall and taken development matters into their own hands. The successful 1966-1986 battle against the Vine Street expressway ramp and the 2000 fight against the building of the Phillies baseball stadium have united the otherwise disparate groups of Chinatown into a community that has claimed the Chinatown area as theirs. Their heightened awareness about city planning issues has created a more inclusive public-minded community

where partisan interests have been at least twice put aside to work for larger common interests. They've won some big battles and they continue to be vigilant; it's clear they know how to pull together at crucial moments and fight the good fight.

During this new era of globalization, where all local fights are also global in dimension, this community of people who have deep local and extensive global insights can guide our understanding of the future. China and Asia are no longer marginal stepchildren to U.S. interests. Rather than being "exotic" and unusual, their experiences are becoming core to the future of this nation. With the rise of Asian economies and interdependencies, using racism in U.S. policies will risk serious negative consequences.

We've got much to learn from these special people and this special place. This is a root experience generally ignored in the media and in universities, yet fundamentally important for all Americans to understand. And this wonderful book is a great place to begin.

John Kuo Wei Tchen
New York University
2004

Goldstein, Jonathan. *Philadelphia and the China Trade, 1682-1846.* University Park, PA: Pennsylvania State University Press, 1978.

Tchen, John Kuo Wei. *New York Before Chinatown: Orientalism and the Shaping of American Culture, 1776-1882.* Baltimore: Johns Hopkins University Press, 1999.

I look back on my childhood and cherish the time that I grew up in Chinatown. Thirty years ago it was a small community. Most of Chinatown occupied four square blocks and all the families knew one another. My parents came to Philadelphia's Chinatown because they knew people from our village in China, Hoy Sun, who arrived in Philadelphia before them. And those that came before them came because they knew people who preceded them.

We lived in three homes over the course of my childhood and all were within the boundaries of Chinatown. The house where I spent most of my youth was not your typical mainstream house,

Essay

John William Chin

A Journey Towards Home: My Work and Roots in Philadelphia's Chinatown

but it was typical for Chinatown. It formerly housed a manufacturing company and was located one building north of the corner of 10th and Cherry Streets. We lived across the street from the fire station, which was then considered the edge of Chinatown. I would hear the sounds of the sirens coming and going at all hours of the day and night. Every Sunday morning, I'd look out the window and be assured to see Fire Ladder 23 parked right in front of my home. The firemen would extend this motorized ladder past the height of my window to do maintenance and then wash the fire truck. Sometimes I'd wave to the fireman climbing that ladder outside my window, three stories high.

The family house was also the family restaurant. My parents worked downstairs in the restaurant sixteen hours a day and came upstairs to sleep, only to repeat the cycle the next day, and the

day after that, and the day after that. Their leisure time began after work in the twilight hours playing mahjong with other friends that worked in the restaurant business. I would wake up after midnight to the clashing sound of hard, plastic tiles that served as mahjong tiles. I would stumble out to see which friends came by to play, mutter some "hello's" to folks, and fall back into my bed since I had school the next morning. When I was younger, I would go to Tuck Hing, the local grocery store, to buy one of my favorite foods, jung, a bamboo leaf rice wrap. They still do have the best.

My mother told me that she sent me to Mitzie's kindergarten school, at the age of three or four, so that she could tend to other responsibilities. I had a new baby brother at home and my mother also helped my father at the restaurant. Mitzie Mackenzie and the Chinese Christian Church and Center were then located on Race Street and now are on 10th and Spring Streets. I attended Holy Redeemer Church down on Vine Street. PCDC (Philadelphia Chinatown Development Corporation), the community organization that I now lead, is an outcome of the grassroots effort to save Holy Redeemer from demolition thirty years ago. In my late twenties I became a volunteer at Holy Redeemer School. That was the beginning of a journey that I continue today as the executive director of PCDC. It opened my eyes to the tremendous need in the community.

Those institutions are still here today to serve a new generation still coming to Chinatown, the gateway for new immigrants, a strong ethnic community with vibrant colors, language, and culture. But the small-town feel is gone and there are many new faces I don't recognize. The streets are bustling with life with the likes of residents, grandparents, preschoolers, delivery people, and tourists.

Chinatown's population is now close to 5,000 people. The population density, the number of restaurants, and the abundance of wholesale food companies servicing the restaurant trade create too much trash, and the odor is unbearable in the summer. The living quarters are shrinking, the open/green space nonexistent, except maybe for Franklin Square, one of William Penn's original four Philadelphia city squares. But Franklin Square is seldom used by the residents of our community. It's dangerous and difficult to cross, the streets wide and heavily traveled. Less transparent are the social and health problems that are not talked about because of cultural values.

Chinatown was the place of opportunity for my parents to test their entrepreneurial skills, to achieve the "American Dream." The skills that earned them a living in their homeland could not put food on our table. The language and cultural barriers were too great. So the building that was our home also provided for us. The family restaurant occupied the first and second floors. In Chinatown it was the norm for families to operate businesses on the ground floor and live above them. Eventually the restaurant put me and my two younger siblings through college.

I look into the eyes of today's immigrants and see my parents and the same issues that confronted them. Our community is experiencing a wave of immigration from Fujian while forty years ago my parent's generation came from Canton (Guangdong). It has taken me four long years to build ten new houses in Chinatown for low-income families. I smile when I think about the ten families that PCDC moved out of substandard housing and into their new homes. But the reality that I struggle with every day as the executive director is that 160 families did not get new housing.

I can get by with my limited Cantonese, so the people I deal with are my tie to my history, my origins. I can't forget the struggles as long I work here, because I see those struggles everyday in the people that I help. Because we straddle two cultures, I'm afraid that my family and I will lose our heritage. I want my young daughter and son to feel—as I do—that Chinatown is their home.

I'm still here, because this will always be my home. It will always be my goal to help the people in my community by creating an environment where new immigrants can flourish as my parents eventually did and by bringing housing, economic development, neighborhood planning, and social issues to the fore. I want every person to have the same opportunities that were afforded me in this community. I want people to be proud of their culture and to feel like they belong in this country. I want to empower residents, ensure the continued growth of Chinatown, and create opportunities for improved education, health, and employment. I have wonderful memories of my childhood. I'll always be grateful to my parents

> **"Chinatown was the place of opportunity for my parents to test their entrepreneurial skills, to achieve the 'American Dream.' The skills that earned them a living in their homeland could not put food on our table. The language and cultural barrier were too great."**

because they made personal sacrifices so that we would have a better life in America. They had help along the way. Now my journey continues.

John Chin
Philadelphia Chinatown Development Corporation
2004

Portraits

I started teaching in 1980. When I first came here, I was the only lay teacher. In time, as the number of available sisters dwindled, lay teachers began replacing the sisters in the classroom. In 1992, they made the difficult decision to withdraw from Holy Redeemer. Their religious community typically went in, started a mission, and left, and another order would take over. But that didn't happen here. They were here for about fifty years. At that point I was asked to take over and step into these big shoes.[1]

Holy Redeemer's always been a gathering place, an important part of Chinatown. On their days off, you'll see our students playing here if their parents are working in Chinatown and they're waiting for them

Lisa Cancelliere

Born January 28, 1959 in Philadelphia, PA.

Lisa Cancelliere is the Principal of Holy Redeemer Chinese Catholic School.

to get off work. We often get calls from people who are driving downtown who say, "Oh, we saw your children walking to school. And they're just so cute." The newspapers want to take pictures. We're glad when we have opportunities to share what and who we are with others on more than just a surface level.

My mother's Japanese and her parents immigrated from Japan. Her family originally settled in California and they lived there until the war. At that time they were placed in an internment camp in rural Arkansas. First they put them in Santa Anita Racetrack where they lived in the stables for six months.[2] During that time, my mother's father died of a stroke. After the war, they decided to settle in Philadelphia largely due to the intervention of the Quakers in Philadelphia while they were in camp. They actually didn't settle in Chinatown but lived in a couple different areas. They started out in West Philadelphia, eventually moving to the Lower Northeast where

we live now. After their experience during the war there was a lot of shame on their part and I think the feeling was to be as "American," as obviously "American," as possible. We were raised in an area where there was one ethnic group. I was more in contact with the Italian half of my background. My father belonged to his parish with his family for a long time so that helped us get accepted. During my childhood, I experienced what many Asians experience. Mostly strangers would make derogatory comments and that was a part of growing up, learning how to deal with that. Our kids experience much of the same thing and it's not an easy thing to deal with, but we try to help them cope with it as best as possible.

I noticed right away that Chinatown stands out as an extremely close-knit community. The Italian American community did have some similarities to this. While we didn't all live in the same neighborhood, we did share a lot of things. Chinatown reminded me a little bit of that, but Chinatown was by far much more concentrated in a small area and much more tight-knit. With Holy Redeemer, there's a deeper kind of relationship than you'd have in most neighborhoods and with most neighborhood schools, most churches even. Someone outside the community may think "that's Chinese" but there's an awful lot of diversity. We have children from all walks of life. In our parish, there's quite a variety of income levels and languages and diversity among the people who come to church here, so we try to serve their needs.

One of the first things I remember in the community was the building of Dynasty Court.[3] I was teaching at the time and it was really something to see that so many people wanted housing here. It was amazing, I've never seen anything like it. They lined up for days outside an office waiting to apply for one of the apartments. They were lined up in the street over night, they were playing mahjong. That really struck me. Wow, what a community and what a need there is here for housing! So many people want to live here.

I was born in China, south China—in Guangdong. When I was six years old, we went to Hong Kong. After about a year, we left Hong Kong, right before Japan attacked and Hong Kong surrendered. I remember for maybe a month, I saw English soldiers patrolling all the streets, we thought maybe they'll stop Japan by force, but they left and Japan landed.[1]

My father was born in California but thought that the United States was very difficult. At that time on the West Coast, it was mostly laundry business, you know; it was cold and because of the cost of living it was not easy to make it, so we stayed in China. My mother had five kids, five boys. I'm number five.

Jong Kai Chin

Born December 7, 1933 in Fung Kwong, Guangdong Province, China.

Jong Kai Chin is a longtime resident and business owner in Chinatown. He is a former president of the Philadelphia chapter of the Gee How Oak Tin Benevolent Association.

My number three brother needed us to come over here, so in 1958 when I was twenty-four, I immigrated to Philadelphia. At this time, airplanes were really slow. I stopped first in Pacific Grand Island and then Hawaii. And then I went to San Francisco. Then Philadelphia. So I think I flew for almost thirty hours. In China I was a student in higher education—I studied Russian—but after I came over, I never got to study English. My brother helped me find a job as a waiter. I came over at 10 p.m. The next day I was already in the restaurant working.

My brother helped me find a job as a waiter and I stayed with this for eight years. Then I applied for a job as a chemical engineer for a chemical corporation in Chestnut Hill. I had an education in Communist China. But it was the Cold War at that time and that chemical corporation did research for the Defense Department.[2]

Although I was a citizen and had a right to apply, after a short time they raised an issue and said that this job was not right for me—maybe it was because I was a minority, maybe because of my background coming from Communist China.

I opened my first business, a restaurant, for ten years, then I got a noodle shop, and opened an import/export company. No time for sleeping. I had two kids already and two more kids were born, very difficult. I had three businesses, you know? Noodle shop, restaurant, grocery, eighteen hour days. Why? My spirit says I can do it. But if somebody looked at me then, I would look sick because I was so skinny. I was 100 pounds, 5 feet 7 inches. If I go swimming, all my ribs were showing.

Now I'm an advisor to this association—the Gee How Oak Tin Benevolent Association has headquarters in San Francisco.[3] There are twenty-eight offices of this association in the United States, Canada, and Mexico. Our association covers three family names—Chin, Wu, Yuan. Our Philadelphia association is about 300 members.

Holy Redeemer School wanted to build a new addition—two classrooms, cafeteria, and library. We are not Catholic but we thought our community has a lot of children studying there so we have a right to help. So I said to Father Tom, "You come to our association's New Year Party, we'll let you speak."[4] Our association donated $3,000, and then personally I gave $6,000. You know why? I had four kids study there. After I did that, everyone, all the associations donated.

Chinatown changes, continues to change. Look at Boston, Los Angeles, San Francisco, New York—big change. But our community changes step by step because we are surrounded on three sides and have no chance to develop. Step by step, but still develop.

I was born in the States, in New York. But after a few months, my parents returned to China so I grew up there. When I went back to my hometown in the countryside, I went to primary school, and then I went out to Guangzhou, Kong Moon, and Hong Kong for eleven years. In China, in the countryside where I grew up, we tended the land, farmed. We weren't poor because my father was here—in the U.S.—and made sure to keep sending money back, which helped build our house, keep up our land, everything.

Wai Lum Chin

Born January 9, 1929 in New York, NY.

Wai Lum Chin, and his wife Janne, lived in Chinatown for many years. Retired from the restaurant business, Wai Lum is a former president of the Philadelphia chapter of the Gee How Oak Tin Benevolent Association in which he and Janne are still actively involved.

Because my first love is eating, this is what I learned. My father was a chef. Starting when I was young, I learned bit by bit and I found it interesting. It's easier to manage a restaurant. Sometimes starting other businesses is difficult since I wasn't experienced and not too educated. Before in Hong Kong and China, I worked many places—on a farm, at a country club. In Philadelphia, I worked in a restaurant as a chef for a few years, then I bought a small restaurant where we worked very hard. Eventually we bought a bigger restaurant called Happy Garden, opposite the fire station. I worked there for ten years and sold it. After a couple of years of relaxing, I got bored and

bought another one. It seems like staying home is not quite comfortable—I need to have something to do or I can't stand it.

When I first came here, restaurants were very rare, there were only about eight or nine at most. Now, year by year, more and more are opening. More people come and there is more business. Now more people come, there are more supermarkets. We have everything, we don't have to go to New York to yum cha.[1]

The most memorable thing from my early days was 9th Street. There were only abandoned houses and a lot of drunks, bars, and homeless people around. On 9th Street, all the abandoned houses were torn down and they rebuilt new houses. I moved to Philadelphia's Chinatown in 1964. I came to the States and worked here for two years, then I returned to get married in Hong Kong. We have three grown children—two sons and one daughter. Nowadays, people can get educated and if there's anything wrong with the government, they will protest. Before, not many people would do that.

Chinatown has been established here for a long time. It was here when we came. Where there is a Chinese person, there will be a Chinatown. Back then, there was a language barrier when Chinese people came to the States. Where there is a Chinatown, Chinese gathered together and could communicate and chat. I feel that it's my home.

Our Chinatown is wonderful. But I hope that Chinatown, narrow Chinatown, would expand and spread into a new Chinatown. More development, more housing—meaning more Chinese people could live there. The more people, the merrier.

I was born in Vietnam. My dad was in the army, we were a wealthy family. When I was nine years old, I left the country. When I first came here, a lot of kids looked at me strangely. But it didn't take much for us to start being friends. I mean, it takes fights to become friends as kids. The language was a problem, but being a kid it wasn't hard for me to pick up the language, the nuances, friendships. I went through school learning English and graduated from college.

When I got to the age of fourteen, I started working. My uncle had an apartment in Norristown, so he rented out the other rooms to chefs at the restaurant. At that time, they needed a dishwasher. My uncle said, "Why don't you take the kid up?" You don't really have much choice. I remember the first day, I was soaking wet from washing

Jayson Choi

| Born June 6, 1971 in Ho Chi Minh City (Saigon), Vietnam.
| Jayson Choi is the owner of Choi Funeral Home in Chinatown.

these dishes. It wasn't a really busy restaurant but I was barely tall enough. I had to stand on the stool to get the hose in, peel onions. It was hot, and I remember that whole ten-hour day was treacherous. I came back and didn't even make it to my room. I fell asleep right in the hallways of the apartment drenched in oil, grease, and water. It was disgusting.

I came back to Philadelphia to start a funeral home. Philadelphia did not have an existing Chinese or Asian funeral home. I went to ask religious figures—monks. I'm excellent at Catholic burials, I know Christian burials. But the Chinese and Vietnamese were Buddhist. So what I concentrated on was learning Buddhist customs. The funeral business is hard to get into. It wasn't easy at all. There's ethnic division. You could say it's racist, but it's not. Blacks stay with blacks, Italians stay with Italians, Irish with Irish. Because of custom. So I put myself everywhere. Banquets, social events, Chinese events.

Everybody. I was walking around introducing myself. Anywhere that was Chinese, I went. I learned who I should talk to, who's the head of this, who's the head of that. You've got to learn all those things. And once I did that, it was good. But it wasn't easy. People don't accept new things in Chinatown really fast. Very superstitious. They were afraid of ghosts, you know. People were saying that I make money off the dead, which is voodoo. Death is really bad luck. I look at it this way: if I'm not going to do it, somebody else is going to do it.

I know this place well. The people. I can walk down the street and see people I've known my whole life. Go into a store or get something to eat. If I don't have any money today, I can just buy something and say I'll pay tomorrow. "OK. OK." I was thinking about buying one of these new condos because, you know, I love this community.[1] It's a cozy community that's growing.

Everything's moving so fast. A lot of times what I learn dealing with these families is that you really have to say what you mean. Just say it. Don't be afraid to say it, communicate with your loved one right there. Before they die, they should talk. With a lot of Asian parents, there's a lack of communication. Either you scream or you don't talk. My father never apologizes. We scream and holler and tomorrow we act like nothing happens. Where we have a problem is that we really do care deeply about each other.

At funeral services, the younger generation doesn't want to be traditional where they have to wear these outfits and kneel. But being in the middle of both sides, I try to match them up. At the end of the funeral, nobody really gets into a screaming match. They come here because they need to communicate and get through the funeral. You see a lot of people who work, work, work. That's a lot of my clientele. They work all their lives and I always think: spend now.

Usually in our village if it was Independence Day or an occasion like that, we would have a dance performance but it was just in the street, you know.[1] We would do Javanese dances but it was funny because I am Chinese but here I was dressing in Javanese clothes, wearing a kebaya.[2]

I would often go home late at night or walk around by myself in Indonesia. Before all the trouble happened, I never felt afraid.[3] But after all the trouble, people became more bold. They started doing things that were a lot worse than just saying rude things. One time I was going with my younger sibling to call my other sibling international so I had to go to the wartel.[4] When we got there, we were

L.D.

Born August 6, 1972 in Kalisat, East Java Province, Indonesia.

L.D. lives and works in Chinatown.

the only Chinese people in the place and this person came up to us and said, "You. You're Chinese, go tell your papa don't lie or you'll find out yourself what will happen." I was frightened. Because of his words and the way he looked—how do I describe it? Serious. Another time I was coming home by myself on a train and there were a couple of guys sitting in front of me. They were talking to me and asked, "Hey, where are you from?" I knew that by asking me, they really wanted to know if I was Chinese or not. I said, "Oh, I live in Java." I said it like that. Then I said, "Yeah, I'm Chinese," and automatically their faces changed. They didn't want to speak to me anymore.

Six years was a long time at one job and I wanted to come to America. I couldn't have both things. It would be impossible—I had to sacrifice one for the other, you know. I wasn't thinking about spending the rest of my life in America. Actually I came here because I met my boyfriend in Philadelphia! But it wasn't an easy decision. I didn't

want to become illegal but I also worried about living in Indonesia because there is discrimination there against Chinese people. In the end, I thought it would be better to live here in Philadelphia where there are a lot of Indonesians. I thought, "America is a big country," so maybe if you don't really know anyone, if there are other Indonesians, even if you don't know who they are, they will help you out.

Before, I was living in this house in Chinatown, I had some happy times. That was when I was living with eight others in one house. We were like a big family, so you felt as if you really weren't alone. If you're sick here, you certainly feel worried because you're here all alone. If you were at home you would have your mom or someone else take care of you. But here, it's your friends who will help you. They'll feed you, take you to the doctor. Also if there's a birthday, you can celebrate together. All these small things make you feel good.

I think 10th Street in Chinatown is good; 8th Street I don't like because it's not that busy. I like it over here, you know—12th, 11th, 10th, it's still a lot of people. Even though it's at night, you still see people walking so you won't feel scared, and I feel that houses here are cleaner than in South Philadelphia. In Chinatown if you want to have a good apartment, it's a little bit more than in South Philadelphia. I know Holy Redeemer has a free clinic here every Thursday. That's good too. Chinatown is an OK place. When I immigrated here there was a protest about whether to make a baseball stadium.[5] I mean people here care more about their neighborhood.

My grandfather was among the railroad pioneers.[1] He built a railroad from Colorado Springs, Colorado, which linked to Oakland where he met a Chinese girl. They got married, settled down in 821 Washington Street in the heart of San Francisco's Chinatown where my father was born.

My father had a laundry at 825 Locust Street and I was born in Jefferson Hospital, 1920.[2] Because of the immigration authorities, Chinese wanted their children to go back to China at an early age so they can get Chinese culture. Immigration laws didn't allow too many Chinese citizens to bring their wives over here.[3] The city of Philadelphia was so big, but there wasn't more than a dozen Chinese women, and one of them was my mother. At the end my mother was considered a big landowner. And, you know, she was executed

Joseph Eng

Born August 8, 1920 in Philadelphia, PA.

Joseph Eng, a retired electrician and World War II veteran, lives in On Lok House, a senior citizens home in Chinatown.

during the Communist Revolution.[4] The immigration law did not open until 1946 when the Second World War was over and my wife was the first group who was free to come over as a G.I. Bride.[5]

I went back to China in July 1922 and stayed over there until January the 5th, 1935. Chinatown was just one block from 9th to 10th, and there was a couple stores before 9th and Race. You could smell beer joints all over. 8th is Metropolitan Hospital now, it used to be called the tenderloin, which had a theater. Ten cents to see two main features, a cartoon, and a coming attraction for a dime. Bars were all over Chinatown. The four corners on 10th and Race were called merry-go-round: you could smell the beer all around. My church was right next to a saloon and, before you went up the steps on 1006 where I went to learn ABCD, you could always smell it.

My father settled down in Camden, New Jersey, where I went to school. Classmates came over and asked me do homework everyday.

But the kids—the boys could come over, I don't know why they didn't let girls come over. It wasn't nice for a Chinese boy to associate with everybody, to have American girls come over to my father's laundry and ask me for homework.

Daytime we went to school and nighttime we came home to work for my father in the laundry. We lived right in the laundry. Right in the back was our bedroom and kitchen. He had four children living there. It was a small laundry. Because of the Depression, nobody was able to get work, money was so tight. We settled down in Camden and we walked. We got two pair of shoes, one was good—to go to church, one was bad—to walk on the bridge. Back and forth, back and forth. Wintertime, it didn't make any difference.

I went to war from beginning to end. I was working for Howard Johnson for a dollar a day. One time a man said, "Hey, that good-looking guy over there. Is he a Japanese?" One of the waitresses said, "Oh, we really love him, he's Chinese, a fine boy." So one of the guys told me to come over and the waitress said, "Hey Joe, come over." I put down the tray and walked over there and the guy shook my hand. I was so surprised! "Didn't you get the news?" He said the Japanese had just declared war on us, they bombed Pearl Harbor.[6] Man, I was shocked.

After I came back from the war, I took the G.I. Bill and went to learn a trade as an electrician.[7] Right after my graduation, the Korean War started. And the Navy Yard, right here—the biggest navy yard in the East—hired me as the first Chinese boy.[8] In 150 years, this is the first Chinese boy to get in there. Last week I went to Carnegie Hall, listened to my great-granddaughter playing a viola and I'm so happy 'cause I look and there's a Lee, a Chou, a Wong, a Lee, so many Chinese boys and girls up on the stage. Now I see that the second generation really has more education, not like it used to be.

So many Chinese come to Philadelphia, into On Lok House, and ask, "When can I come in here?"[9] If you build another one, it's still not enough. It's very difficult. Chinatown cannot go west, east, south, the only thing that we can get out is north of Vine Street. Our Chinatown is so crowded, ten kids together at one room. I'm glad everybody in Chinatown get together, fight so hard for "No Stadium in Chinatown."[10] And I would like to see more homes on the north of Vine Street for the youngsters to see some dream—something started on the other side of Vine Street.

We've been visiting Chinatown since I was born. Though my parents lived in West Philadelphia, they socialized here. If you wanted to eat Chinese food, there was only one place to go. All their friends socialized, worshipped, did grocery shopping in Chinatown. My earliest memory of it was when I was a child coming down for Chinese New Year's Eve being so bundled up I could barely see what was going on. I distinctly remember the smell of sulfur, boom of firecrackers, and hearing the clanging chimes and the lion dance. My father talks about his first days in Philadelphia walking around with ten dollars in his pocket, not knowing many people wandering

Catharine Fan

Born April 8, 1966 in Philadelphia, PA.

Catharine Fan is a parishioner at Holy Redeemer Catholic Church and the Community Relations Officer for the Philadelphia Police Department, 6th District, which covers Chinatown.

around Chinatown, specifically Race Street. It was just filled with signs. Back then, in the early 1960s, you would have a restaurant, a house, restaurant, laundromat, a couple homes. He really felt, with that mixture of commercial and residential, that he was in the streets of Taipei.

Ever since I was a little girl, I used to watch those cop shows— *Starsky and Hutch, Police Woman, Charlie's Angels*. It seemed really exciting—shooting, car chasing, that kind of stuff. As I got older, my parents emphasized education, definitely not law enforcement. No police work, it's not good to have people shoot at you all the time. My parents chose to leave their homeland to come to the United States because they wanted a better life for their children so the last thing they wanted was their daughter to be a police officer. But as I got older, I realized there's a lack of resources available to certain

members of the community. In our country, we tend to feel that if someone does not speak English, or understand it, they are not intelligent, and it's not true. When I was applying for the Department back in the late 1980s, the Southeast Asian immigrant explosion was overtaking the Northeast corridor.[1] We were the fifth largest city in the nation and we had no Southeast Asian speakers. I noticed then that most of the Chinese-speaking officers spoke Cantonese, not Mandarin. And with the sudden flow of new arrivals from Fujian province, they speak only Fukienese or Mandarin.[2] Less than ten police officers in this Department who can speak Mandarin and understand it, even fewer who can read and write it. I'm lucky, I came in at the right time.

My main responsibility is to foster a positive relationship between community groups and this particular district. I hate for anyone in this district to feel that they can't talk to the police, because that's what I'm here for. What I love about this job is meeting people, all the time. All kinds of people. The fact is that this area alone is a perfect example of what the world is.

I have a friend who lives over on 200 Camac Street.[3] From her rooftop, you can see the Convention Center.[4] The other way, she sees City Hall. When we were younger, and it was a hot summer night and you wanted to get a cool breeze, we would climb to her roof, have some lemonade and beer, try to look at the stars but not be able to. We would say, "Wow, from where your house is situated, you would never know people live underneath the shadows of all those great structures." But we're one of the few communities situated smack in the center of a major commercial area. You have all these large structures but interspersed are homes.

When people eventually get around to asking, "Where do you work?" and I tell them I work in Chinatown, they say, "Oh, what's it like?" I say that Chinatown is not like what they picture in those movies with the steam and neon signs, like Eddie Murphy in that movie *Trading Places* where it looks really mysterious. Chinatown is not like that. Chinatown is bursting with life and energy. Everybody has a different story to tell, everybody has a sad tale and a happy tale. The best thing about Chinatown is the people. The fact that over 100 years, it's still here. We can't say that about a lot of things in this country, even in this city.

My father died in 1960 when China had what's called the "three years' difficult period."[1] Many peasants and farmers died because there was no food. Most laboring men died so my father died at that time. My mother, my elder sister, and I lived together. My mother died three years ago. She died at eighty-one years old. I still remember her. My mother worked very hard. She brought me and my elder sister up. It wasn't easy in the countryside. I was born in Anhui province, in China. I had a very hard time in the countryside to tell you the truth. In the middle of the Great Cultural Revolution, the Chinese government decided to send students who had not graduated from school to the countryside to work with peasants.[2] Everyone went to factories to

Bihong Guan

Born December 26, 1948 in Xuanchen village, Anhui Province, China.

Bihong Guan, a real estate broker and acupuncturist, is President of the Greater Philadelphia United Chinese American Chamber of Commerce from 1997 until 2005.

work, then after three or four years the government decided we needed education so they selected workers and peasants from each unit.

I was elected by our township. My middle school was one of the sixty best in China. We all lived in a dormitory. We took classes and also farmed. In China, you have to help farm to understand how hard the peasants, or workers, worked. If you don't work, you know nothing, you just know knowledge.

Thirteen years ago when I came to Philadelphia, to Chinatown, I was very nervous because I didn't know anybody. From Temple University to Chinatown, at that time I want to save some money. I just walked that long distance to Chinatown to buy some rice, some eggs, some tomatoes and carrots, and walked home, carrying my purchases to Temple, Cooney Hall. At that time, I lived in Cooney Hall. I didn't know anybody.

At the beginning, I planned to go back. Even after finishing my master's degree—I got my master's from Temple—I was planning to go back. Then I brought my family, my wife and son, to go to Europe to travel, a lot of countries. If I went back to China, it would be hard for me to find a chance to go to Europe. But the Tiananmen Square incident happened. So President Bush, Sr., signed a notice to let all Chinese students stay here giving them a green card, permanent residency. Thirty thousand Chinese students chose to stay here and I was in that group.[3]

It's not easy for foreigners, especially when your English is not so perfect. Even though I was a teacher at the university teaching English, I had no chance to practice. So when I first came here, I sat in the classroom and felt it was very difficult to understand what the professor was lecturing. My degree was in psychology then, in counseling psychology, but I didn't take the license test. I thought no Americans would come to me for psychological counseling. Chinese, Asian people usually don't go to psychologists for mental problems. They usually just overcome them by themselves.

In 2000, we fought against Mayor John Street.[4] Also we fought inside Chinese community because it is not so united. A big fight in the newspapers because I wrote an article against Street's decision to build a baseball stadium in Chinatown. Some people said, "You cannot represent us." I said, "I represent my organization. I didn't represent you." So we had a big fight in our newspaper, our community. Finally we got together.

In 1996, I had a party in my new house with some students just like me from Temple. We should have an organization to get together. We thought during that time it was strange here that the old residents, the Chinese, Chinatown, nobody celebrated the National Day of the People's Republic of China—the People's Republic of China was founded October 1, 1949. I come from mainland China, Communist China. Here they only celebrate Ten Ten Day, shuang shih.[5] Double Ten, you see. We think this situation should be changed, so we agreed to organize to establish the Greater Philadelphia United Chinese American Chamber of Commerce. So in 1997 we had some friends, got together, and first thing on October 1st, we had a big celebration at Independence Park, raised the flag of the People's Republic, and had a parade.

The time I grew up in the 1950s was tough. My mom and dad had a tough time earning a living. I started school late, at nine years old. At that time children were not guaranteed an education. Chinese people consider sons more important than daughters. I have an elder brother and two younger brothers so my mom first sent my elder brother and then my younger brothers to school.

We didn't do much on weekends. On weekends, my mom made us wipe the table, drawers, chests, and wall—clean house. Because our family was not wealthy, we just stayed at home and watched TV. For Hong Kong youngsters back in my time there wasn't much—boat rowing, bike cycling. Nowadays, people car race—back then we

Wai Man Ip

Born in Hong Kong, China.

Wai Man Ip is a resident and owner of three stores in Chinatown: Chinese Cultures & Arts, Asia Crafts, and China Art Company. We also interviewed her son, Eric, for the Oral History Project.

bicycle raced! You could go from Hong Kong Island, to Kowloon and back full round, that's how small Hong Kong is.[1] I grew up in Kowloon but I frequently went over to Hong Kong Island, just across the harbor. I always went there to play. To go eat. We all really liked the Hong Kong side.

I came to America right after I got married and it was really different. Upon arriving, I couldn't go out too much, because I didn't feel well, and I didn't like eating anything here because I felt that everything wasn't fresh, the fish and everything else was all frozen. Chinatown at that time was really very barren. The buildings were all dilapidated, some were just old. There were very few shops. I could remember only three: Huen Cheong, Tuck Hing, and Hong Kee. As for restaurants there were nine or ten. The largest ones were Ho Sai Gai and Lung

Mun. Chinatown was so small. Back then the majority of Chinese restaurants catered to American customers because there were not many Chinese people. Usually people from offices came down to eat.

Not long after I arrived in the States, in 1979, we started our first bookstore. It was a very small bookstore. There wasn't much to sell, mainly magazines from Hong Kong. We hoped that people who worked in the restaurants and didn't speak English would buy some Chinese magazines and newspapers to read when they were bored. They might learn something about happenings in the world. Later *Sing Tao* learned that we were selling magazines in Philly.[2] They were interested in doing business, saw our bookstore, and asked us if we would be interested in becoming their sole agent in Philadelphia. They had papers sent in every day from New York. We were the first to distribute their paper.

At the end of the Vietnam War, many Vietnamese Chinese immigrated here.[3] At that time, Chinatown was very prosperous because the Vietnamese Chinese were used to shopping in the streets. When they first came here, they didn't know English, so on Saturdays and Sundays they all rushed to Chinatown—to buy groceries, buy rice, or flour, in bags of all sizes. I was really happy when I saw this happening. There were so many Chinese. All of Chinatown started to change. After people had been here for some time, things became stable. Among those people who made some money, some wanted to start businesses. So they came to Chinatown to start them.

Many people said that Chinatown in Philly was a wasteland. But Philly is peaceful. Of course, if you like prosperity, you might prefer New York's more rapid pace. But Chinatown in Philadelphia is not far from other places. I've been here for over twenty years. I think Chinatown is very good for me. I'm working here and living here. I feel comfortable here.

My youngest son Eric can speak Chinese, yes, because we talk to him in Cantonese. He learns Chinese in school too. But he learns Mandarin. He knows a little bit. Right now we live in Chinatown, he is happy to live here because his friends are in Chinatown. I want to send him out for college. He doesn't want to go. He wants to stay at home. I tell him, "You'd better go out as far as you can now."

In 1979 when we first came over, it was hard to adjust because it was totally new for us and we felt like a new child just born. Crossing from Vietnam to the United States, when you get to the South China Sea it's like your life is cut in half: fifty percent of you lives, fifty percent dies.

In Vietnam my father organized people to escape the country.[1] He got caught and they released him from jail nine months later. The government gave us permission to leave, escorted us out to sea, and we just went from there. We hit one of the oil tankers in the middle of the ocean. That's how they provided us with more oil and food. The sea was getting too dangerous and one of the tankers transferred all the women and children to the big ship. The men had to stay on this

Benny Lai

Born May 26, 1967 in Saigon Cho Lon District, Vietnam.

Benny Lai and his family own Vietnam restaurant in Chinatown.

little boat to Malaysia because they were afraid they might hijack the ship. The island, what the refugee camp was called, I forget the name of it. I was little.

When we came, we were on welfare and we started working for cash under the table. In the summer we went over to pick blueberries in Jersey. They have buses that park on 46th and Walnut—at four o'clock in the morning, they start loading Asian blueberry pickers. So we went there. My dad was working as a truck deliverer in New York. Welfare provided us with just enough for food and rent. That's it. We needed extra cash to buy clothing and transportation.

There was this one grocery store in Chinatown. We were immigrants and they noticed that. My mom and I walked in the store and you could see the whole family come out watching us, saying, "Oh, we should watch them because they may steal." My family—we're

Chinese—we understand what people say. In the beginning we felt so bad. We wore free clothing that we got from church. Nothing matched, your shoe was a half size bigger, you wore pink, a girl color, but who cares? You have something to put on. The jacket is oversized, it'll hang down to your knees. But they're free clothes so you can't ask more than that. We felt great. We had something to wear. Because when you're in refugee camp, you get nothing but two sets of clothes, wash one and one dry.

Every night my uncle would bring home leftovers from the restaurant. That was what we ate—the meat still stuck on the bone. My older brother was a dishwasher at Imperial Inn. I was dishwasher at the Chinese restaurant on Penn's campus. The dishwasher position, it's professional. You stand there with steam coming out. All the water you stick your hands in feels like a firehose. Keep doing it again. They used cheap detergent, made you wash your hands. I came home with a rash on my skin. Back then the only position open was dishwasher. You don't need to speak English. Go to your bucket, that's it. Just clean it and bring it out. That's why I treat my kitchen staff professional.

My dad wanted to start a Vietnamese restaurant in Chinatown. I remember when we first opened that we had Caucasian people walk in, the whole dining room is full of Vietnamese and Asian, and stop. For two seconds. Before people thought Vietnamese food was raw food because when they watched the news, all they showed was the jungle and the G.I.s that died. They didn't show the city.

I think around in 1985-1986, I saw a lot more Vietnamese immigrants in Chinatown. Some of them started businesses. We had six Vietnamese restaurants in Chinatown from 1984 to 1989. Today in Chinatown it reminds me of back then when we got flooded by the Vietnamese community—now we have Chinese immigrants called Fuzhou, from Fujian province.[2] They've almost taken over the whole of Chinatown because there's so many of them. That's why you see a lot of businesses and new stores popping up.

Chinatown is my home. This is the Chinatown that helped us get back to our feet. People always recognize me, say hi. Not like before. Even the people that said those things in the grocery store, I see them now and we always talk to each other and they pay us more respect than before.

I was born at Jefferson Hospital.[1] I grew up in Chinatown, lived there all my life. My mom owns three stores in Chinatown. My brother owns his own store and my sister works at an insurance place. And my other two sisters go to school.

Many people that come here, they come from China or anywhere else, to Chinatown to live throughout the years. They work up, like my grandpa. In Chinatown, actually right now, it is mostly Fukienese people and then there is Cantonese people and then a whole bunch of different Chinese people. I'm not sure if it's correct or not, but I think my grandpa went to Cuba first. And then he came to New York.

Eric Law

Born January 20, 1985 in Philadelphia, PA.

Eric Law graduated from Central High School and now attends Penn State. He lives in Chinatown with his siblings and mother, Wai Man Ip.

And then he just came down to Chinatown, Philadelphia, because New York was crowded or something. I think he stayed here and worked here for some years. And then I don't know how he did the process, but he got my dad and my grandma to come over. My grandpa, he always had a restaurant in Chinatown. And then they worked in there. My grandpa is still living in Chinatown.

Society at large thinks the whole area is just restaurants. They come in to eat, but it's just like any other neighborhood in Philadelphia—we just have a lot more restaurants. But underneath that it's people growing up, their daily lives. When I was little, we would be playing in the streets. We used to do stupid stuff, we'd pick up cans from the floor, on the ground and put them right in the middle of the street and watch cars run by it. We didn't have anything to do. And we

used to play football and basketball and hockey. There's a time too when we were killing slugs with salt.

When I would go to school, the other kids would always say, "I had meatloaf for dinner," or, "Oh, I had pizza for dinner." I'm like, "I want some of that." When I go home, I have rice with fish and stuff. I thought maybe I should go ask someone and go somewhere else to eat. I would always beg my mom to take us to Pizza Hut or go get some cheesesteak or something.

I think when I started doing the lion dances for the Philadelphia Suns, it got me more into Chinese culture.[2] We used to do shows for people and I was happy. At Chinese New Year, when we had the big parade, it was great because we had all these lion heads around and firecrackers exploding. Besides basketball, we hang out, talk, play cards. There's a basketball court and a playground inside Chinese Christian Church.[3] The playground opens during the summer and we play, sit around and play board games.

It's important to me to point out where I'm from because it's the basis of who I am. That's where I'm from, that's where I've lived my whole life. It's part of me. It's important—holding on to where you're from, your ancestors. Because before in eigth grade, I hated Chinese culture. I thought: "I don't want to do this. I don't want to be F.O.B."[4] Back then, well, still now today, there were a lot of recent immigrants in Chinatown. And I didn't hate them but they were just different from me, so I thought, "Alright, I don't want to be grouped with them," so I just pushed myself away from them, the Chinese side, into American culture. Most of them didn't speak English and they actually spoke a different dialect of Chinese, Fukienese. I spoke English all the time, hung out with white and black friends more. But as I grew older, I thought, "You know what? Maybe I should stop being something I'm not, you know?" So with my baby cousins, I always talk Chinese to them and say a little English 'cause they don't live in Chinatown, they live in the suburbs. I try to help them, or something.

My family grew tobacco. In China, old people like to use square paper to roll tobacco. When I was six years old, I helped my family harvest. I watched our cows to make sure they turned the soil loose and put tobacco seeds inside there. At twelve, I harvested those tobacco plants with cutting tools.

I lived with my family until I got married. My husband and I got married but he was in the United States. I was pregnant and I stayed with my daughter in the country, in China—Hoksahn district in Guangdong. He came here first and then applied for me and my daughter to come to the U.S. when I was around fifty-three years old. That's why I only had one daughter. I needed to stay at my husband's family's place to help farm,

Chun Moy Lee

Born January 6, 1912 in Lamtou, Guangdong Province, China.

Chun Moy Lee, called Chut Po, is a volunteer lunch lady at Holy Redeemer Catholic School. She is considered by many to be the "great-grandmother of Chinatown."

harvest, and cut those plants. I stayed with my husband's family, more than ten people around two tables. I cooked big bowls of rice so everybody could eat together, because we were farmers, so we needed more rice to fill up our strength and energy to work on the farm until China changed to Communism. Me and my daughter were female workers, members of the Communist Party, but my husband wanted to apply for us to come to the U.S. so that's why we went first to Hong Kong.[1] We then came to the U.S. to be cashiers at Wah Nam Chinese Restaurant in Chinatown, which some of my husband's relatives owned. Wa Nam was located on 9th Street. I didn't want to work at the restaurant. Instead I worked on Arch Street, at a factory, making earrings for ten years.

My granddaughter studied at Holy Redeemer School.[2] My five grandchildren all studied here. Five of them—four boys and one girl—all at Holy Redeemer. I quit my job at the earring factory and came to Holy Redeemer. I've been working here twenty-four years because my granddaughter wanted somebody to be the lunch lady to help the cafeteria. But my granddaughter said there's no salary and I said, "That's okay." I wanted to help because that would make me feel more happy and comfortable. I don't go many places. I go to volunteer at the church mostly, but sometimes I follow other old people to Atlantic City to go gambling. We pay ten dollars to go to the casino and they give us free lunch. I don't buy anything because my daughter buys everything for me. Clothes, food. My daughter is sixty-five this year.

Everything's so cheap in Chinatown. That's why I saved a lot of money. It's so cheap and my husband told me not to go out to work. He worked here a long time already, had some money saved for me to enjoy the rest of my life. I used to work in Hong Kong so my husband told me not work here but I still went out to get a job, to work. I'm a person who works very hard and I can't just sit down and eat. That's the reason I like to work up to right now.

When I met my husband again, we were an old couple already. We were separated for a long time. And that's why I'm very happy, because I came to the United States to see my husband again. I came to Chinatown and everybody here calls me Chut Po. I'm really happy that everybody knows me. I had a birthday party at Imperial Inn on the second floor, the dining room. More than 200 people came to the party. This year I've come to Philadelphia around forty-eight years, and I know a lot of people so that's why 200 people came.

My father is from Guangdong, China. He escaped from the Communist government, went to Hong Kong, stayed there for eight years. He's a teacher and an artist, supported himself to get through English school and his masters program. Then he met my mom when they were in Italy studying abroad.

When I was little, I remember going to Hong Kee's grocery. It's closed down now and he's retired, but my dad used to be really good friends with him. We would go in and they would give us candy. I just remember following my dad around as a little kid, not being able to speak Chinese: "Dad, don't go anywhere, don't leave me."

Romana Lee

Born September 2, 1978 in Doylestown, PA.

Romana Lee works as the Director of Development for the Philadelphia Chinatown Development Corporation (PCDC).

I remember the New Year's parade coming through Race Street and the firecrackers always so loud. We used to run into the store and hide. I was so scared.

When I was growing up, my dad would speak a little bit to us, but I think he really wanted us to be able to speak English well, so from the time I was five till the time I was thirteen, he didn't speak Chinese to us at all. The only times I heard Cantonese were when we would visit his friend's family. And I didn't really hear Toisan until my relatives from San Francisco came to help with our restaurant when I was seventeen.[1] My senior year was the first year we opened and my dad really needed help, so everyday I'd come. I was so busy because I was swimming, I had 5:45 a.m. practice, full day of school, afternoon practice, then do my homework, practice violin, go to orchestra, go to work at the restaurant. My dad asked me, "Why are you so tired?"

"Because I've been at work for eighteen hours, leave me alone." Watching my father really helped me to see how Asian Americans are pigeonholed into doing one kind of work. In Chinatown, there aren't too many different opportunities. Just open a restaurant, accumulate capital from family, friends, borrow money. What really drove me nuts is that my dad did have the education, the language skills, but when it came down to it, to put his children through college, he had to revert to the only way he knew how to make a living that was stable. It's hard for me to watch him. He would really love to be doing art. Anytime my dad has had to support himself, he's gone back to the restaurant business. The current restaurant that my family has is in Lansdale, which is an hour outside of Center City. It's a blue-collar town, not really the best place for the kind of business that he wanted to do, because he wanted to have it be modern Chinese cuisine that exhibited art.

Chinatown's gotten a lot more commercial since 1999 when I first started work, which is a good thing, because it means more business opportunities for newer immigrants. As far as population goes, I notice there are a lot more Mandarin-speaking people and I wonder where they all live, because during the weekdays it's just people who have lived here for years, the older people who are rooted in this community. On the weekends, you have a whole other group of people—tourists and suburban Chinese families. Tourism is good for the community but I want people to recognize that Chinatown's a neighborhood and not just a business community. We are not just made up of restaurants! I really hope people would just respect it, know this is a home.

The summer I interned with PCDC while I was still a college student, I really grew a heart for the community, saw their needs, saw the struggle, the injustice, and ever since that time, I've been with PCDC.[2] I was an international relations major at Tufts and really active in the Asian American community. I did all these things and really felt like that's where my community is, where I found myself. As a biracial person, I don't know how else to describe it, but this is where my heart is, this is where my passion is.

My father passed away when I was ten. My family wasn't rich but we could still make ends meet. I still had my mother. She worked really hard to raise the three of us. I learned Chinese for six years—from when I was seven till when I was twelve. Later I began to learn Malaysian, which was Malaysia's national language.[1] I learned many languages mixed together—Chinese, English, Malaysian.

There's an exam in Malaysia. Passing it will enable you to enter school. If you fail, you're free to choose other options. Because I failed, I chose to find a job and learn things about society. Since I had to work, I worked in more than one place and I have been to many places in Malaysia, almost all thirteen states in Malaysia. I worked, adapted to different environments, and made new friends.

Wei Yew Lee

Born April 8, 1978 in Ipoh, Perak State, Malaysia.

Wei Yew Lee (Leslie) worked as a waiter in Penang Restaurant in Chinatown.

When I was still in school, I worked part-time at a furniture factory. Then my first full-time job was in Singapore after graduation. It was very convenient to come and go between the two countries—only a passport is necessary. I had been out of school, worked for a while, made some money, and my friend who worked with me in Singapore was back in Malaysia and asked me to drop out and work with him in the outside world. My mother was very disappointed when I didn't go back to school. But I believe there should be no regrets, there was no other path for me to choose.

I worked as a steel worker for almost two years. Sometimes I waited two weeks for jobs to come. I stayed at home idle. My mother saw the situation and said, "How about you try your luck by going abroad?" My aunt had been in the States for almost eight or nine years. She had asked my mother to come to the United States before.

My mother thought we were too young at the time, so she didn't go. Since I had grown up, it might be the right time for me to go and find a job in the States. I flew to the United States as soon as I had a visa. I came alone. I was lucky because at least my aunt was here. She lived in New York. I lived there for a few days and then came to Philadelphia to work.

At first it was difficult because I was all by myself. I was worried. It was hard to get used to. First, the working hours in Malaysia were not so long, not twelve hours. Maybe it was tougher there, but the working hours were shorter. I had more personal time. But in the States, it's difficult, twelve hours. The restaurants in Chinatown require, you have to work twelve hours. In order to get into them, you have to work overtime. But the restaurant I work in is good. This restaurant provides both food and lodging. You don't have to worry about food and a place to stay, but it was still difficult to get used to.

It's not been a long time since I came here to Chinatown, just a year or two. More and more people come to Chinatown, it's more and more prosperous as time passes. To me, Chinatown in Philadelphia is peaceful and convenient, ten times better than New York's. I take Philadelphia as part of my life. I'm already here, I will have to adjust to life here, and find what I need here. I can't go back to Malaysia because I haven't made enough yet, but it's hard to say. I have a girlfriend now and we both hope to establish a family in Malaysia, but it's very likely we will have different ideas one day.

My friends are the all the people I got to know at work. Some are introduced to me by friends. They get to know each other because they work away from home. Although they are Malaysian Chinese, they are different. I have many good friends in Chinatown. Wherever you go, when you get familiar with a place, you will have friends. I have found some real friends who know my heart.

It's kind of funny. I have grown up and turned back to the area I grew up in as far as working, as far as serving. The Chinese Christian Church and Center playground is where I grew up.[1] My parents' building was adjacent to the playground so we would pretty much go every-day, whenever it wasn't rainy. As far back as I can remember, my family has been attending this church, my grandmom was very active. When she came to the States, our family, on my grandmom's side, half the kids were committed to the Catholic Church and half the family was here at this Church. I went to McCall School and I taught there as well.[2] I grew up participating with the Philadelphia Suns, a youth group

Harry Leong

Born April 28, 1978 in Philadelphia, PA.

Harry Leong, born and raised in Chinatown, is the current Director of the Chinese Christian Church and Çenter and leads the Philadelphia Suns as a volunteer.

in the community, and later I did some coaching and, about eleven years ago, I had the group incorporated. So my path just ended up beginning at one point and returning back to that one point.

During the 1970s, there was a filmmaker who did a film on Chinatown. We were kids, helping him out, we lugged the cameras around for him. The film had to do with the Vine Street Expressway. This was the 1970s and it was a pretty big thing because we had major events every weekend: filming, going to court, going to hearings. Major protests. Then there was a centennial celebration of Chinatown—I think it was 1971.[3] That was a big event because the community was really working together to celebrate and they closed off all the streets in Chinatown and there was a huge fair.

When we were growing up, the restaurant work was primarily Chinese in the kitchens doing every kind of work and occasionally blacks were hired to work in the kitchens. In the last five years, there's a growing influence of Mexicans, of Hispanics in the area, and they'll take on any kind of job—usually it ends up being the really hard jobs. Whatever the owners don't want to do, they pass it on to the "low man on the totem pole" and it's Hispanics who are at the low end right now.[4]

Another church in the community, Holy Redeemer, had youth teams and participated in various tournaments.[5] There was a new group in 1972-1973, teenagers, and they wanted to form their own team and came up with this name, Philadelphia Suns.[6] They primarily played basketball and did lion dancing as a fundraising thing but continued to participate in Asian basketball leagues across the East Coast.[7] We had, through the Suns, various coaches that helped us along. These guys were our "older brothers," fifteen older brothers. Mitzie was also a mentor, growing up, she watched after us, we were street kids, pretty much.[8]

I definitely feel there is a level of camaraderie when people speak the same dialect, like when we went to San Francisco—San Francisco's more of an older Chinatown and most of the people there are actually Toisanese.[9] When I was growing up, we were often ridiculed because I would go to the stores and order things and because they were Cantonese, they would make fun of my different dialect, say, "Oh, look at that Toisan boy!" or, "Jook sing, jook sing, jook sing."[10]

I wouldn't call myself an ABC.[11] I was born and raised in the community, that would probably tell who I am. I am a product of the community, having grown up here and continuing to be here. I feel like I stake a greater claim to this area because I haven't moved, this is my home. I'm willing to move, but if this is where I am for now—it's like the saying, "Bloom where you're planted." I feel like this is where I'm planted so I'm going to try to bloom.

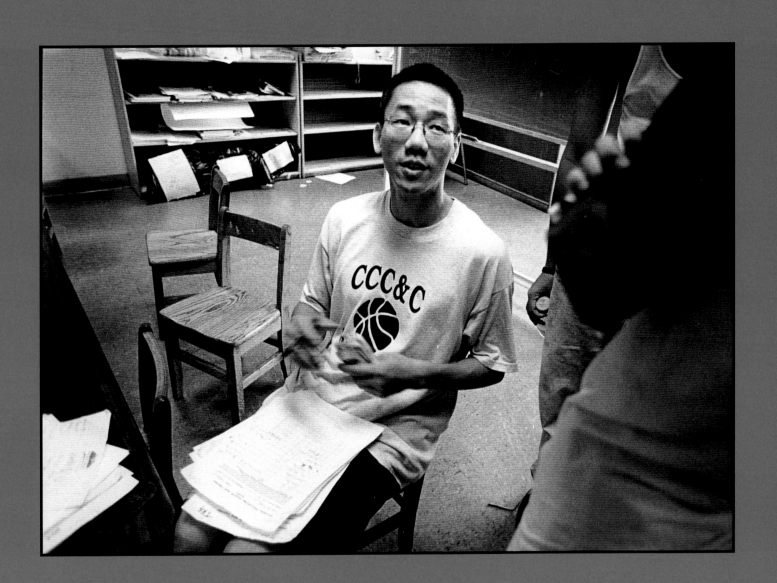

I was born and raised in South Philly. I was eighteen, getting my Master's at Temple University, when I came down to Chinatown. Chinatown didn't wake up until at least noon then. Ms. Scott, the woman who hired me, said I could continue to go to school in the morning and early afternoon then go down to the Center afternoon and evening. She paid me twenty-five dollars every two weeks and helped pay my tuition. That was a good bit then. But it wasn't a lot.

I already knew some of the young Chinese people especially a dear young woman, a classmate at Girls High. One day she passed me a note under the lunch table; she's sixteen and she said, "I have something to tell you. I'm going to get married." Sixteen was young to get

Mitzie Mackenzie

Born August 9, 1920 in Philadelphia, PA.

Mitzie Mackenzie has been an integral part of the Chinese Christian Church and Center for over sixty years where she worked as Center Director. She is working on her autobiography, "Between Tears and Laughter: A History of Chinatown."

married. I still keep in touch with her family. When I first came here, she said, "When I go visiting, you come with me, follow me in and meet people." You know, like that. Because I did that, I've never felt like a stranger, I always felt at home.

Momma always said, "When one door closes, another one opens." It's true. After graduation I got a letter saying, "Would you mind going down to Chinatown and start something?" So I was given the key to 1006 Race Street which used to be a Chinese mission Sunday school. There were Chinese Sunday schools all around Philadelphia then. My mission was to make them Americans. The first thing we did was have a girls club where they learned how to cook American dishes to introduce to their parents. Their parents were from China and they were American. Some of the girls won the American Legion award in their schools.[1]

At that time, there were only twenty families living in Chinatown and 400 men. They were called bachelors, but they weren't really bachelors—they were sojourners who were young when they came and had already married in China before they came over.[2] I started September 8, and the war started December 7, 1941.[3] During the war, we had about forty American girls and one boy because all the boys were in the service. The guys weren't allowed to be citizens but could be if they were in the army. There were 108 Chinese men, some nearing forty, who went into the army to become American citizens.

The Church and Center incorporated in 1946 because we wanted to own property at 10th and Spring Streets. It was a parking lot that we used as a money source until we were able to build our church in 1952. I was called director of activities but in the 1950s, I became director. From 1991 to 1996, I retired but continued to volunteer until the new director came. After that I became director emeritus.

When the Chinatown Gate was built in 1984-1985, a group from China came over.[4] They all wore blue jackets. They came in the spring and said they'd be back in China for Chinese New Year. They had an apartment on 10th and Arch and we provided them with a cook. They said they didn't want any more American food. Before going back we gave them a little money to buy things to take home. They bought pantyhose. After they left we went to clean the apartment. On the floor were piles of papers from pantyhose packages and mounds of cigarette butts.

Chinatown needed housing in the 1970s, desperately. We need it now too. PCDC built housing across the Center called Dynasty Court.[5] I would like to see the area from Vine and Spring Garden developed.[6] There are a lot of old factories, you know, that could be made into affordable places to live. We have to go somewhere, north. Oh, I would love to see that! I'd like to see more places where the young people can have a little space to move. In the summer time when we have our playground open till 11 o'clock at night. The police captain told us that it really kept kids off the street.

I've always been kind of different, I haven't gone around preaching. In fact, I think sometimes the Church wonders what I'm doing. I've always tried to share my faith by living it.

I am actually an Indonesian of Chinese descent. My great-grandmother was native Chinese but we lived in Indonesia for decades. There are a lot of Chinese people in Indonesia and a lot who have businesses there. We had problems because of that issue—race—and the economy was down too.[1] In Indonesia after 1965, Chinese schools and culture were no longer allowed and we could not use Chinese names.[2] We look Chinese, people say we are Chinese, but Chinese people themselves are sometimes wary of us, because we don't speak Mandarin, and our names are different.

Iwan Santoso

Born July 15, 1974 in Malang, East Java Province, Indonesia.

Iwan Santoso's family owns Indonesia Restaurant in Chinatown and Café Pandawa 5 in South Philadelphia.

In 1996, in the the Indonesian community, there were only twenty people, so I was in the first group here, there weren't that many back then.[3] At that time, my relatives had come here before me. Philadelphia has a large work sector which doesn't require high education, too much English—just enough to get by is fine. We looked for work in Chinatown then, because our English was limited, as was our experience. So mostly we worked as dishwashers. Eventually we moved up. We spoke more English which meant that we could work as salespersons. From there, we learned and moved to restaurants where I used more English. At that time, I found work at a cheesesteak shop at Allegheny. Then I worked at a liquor store. Finally I found work at Reading Terminal Market where I worked in a poultry shop for two years, cutting up chicken parts and then finally decided to move on.[4]

Then I worked as a driver taking Indonesian factory workers to factories because I had a driving license and could speak English a little bit. For the first two years we didn't know if we wanted to stay in America, or go home. At that time we only worked here to earn money to take home, but after we got used to living in America, to go back to Indonesia after six years, it would be a big change. We sometimes got tired of working with other people. My parents and I, we decided to start this business. Generally the Indonesian community was growing and they were hard-pressed to find a place, or a restaurant, that specialized in Indonesian food in Philadelphia.

Indonesians aren't really accustomed to the lifestyle here. In Indonesia, even though the economy isn't great, their lives are better than the way we're living now. Stores close at eleven o'clock at night and everything's cheap. In America, the only time for activities are Saturdays when people maybe go to Chinatown, walk around the area. Then during Sundays, the main place to get together is church.[5] That's about it.

It's difficult to get into Chinatown. To work in Chinatown, for Indonesians, we need Mandarin, and not all Indonesians can speak Mandarin. For those of us who don't speak it, it's hard to work in Chinatown. And if there is work, it is heavy, because it may be in the kitchen, or wherever. We can live here, but to communicate, or be social, it is too difficult for us.

Most Indonesians in America must be mentally strong. Getting an American visa is so hard now. In the months following September 11, work was very slow and many Indonesians here were unemployed, so they were frightened about coming and not having a job.[6] A lot of people also have gone home.[7] But for every one person that goes home, there are more that come here.

I was just a boy growing up and everything revolved around the bakery because that's our business. Working at the bakery. Cracking eggs, making the dough. Those are my memories. I know a lot of kids from the church, Holy Redeemer. Playing sports, playing in the playground. I grew up in North Philly, towards the Northeast neighborhood. It was fair, got progressively worse as I grew up. Right now it's pretty urbanized. I would say it's low socio-economic background. And the schools weren't that great. I didn't get the greatest foundation growing up, but we survived.

Khai Tang

Born January 29, 1979 in Philadelphia, PA.

Khai Tang, a pharmacist, lives in Chinatown. His parents own Trung Viet China Bakery and live in Chinatown.

My parents came shortly before I was born. They came from Saigon. They were Chinese from Vietnam. They had to escape like most others.[1] They had to escape Vietnam, came over with practically nothing, just, you know, the shirts on their backs. My father first started waiting tables in Chinatown in the restaurant previously known as King's Restaurant and my mother was a cashier, but this is a long time ago. She also worked at another Chinese restaurant until eventually they opened up the bakery. At that time we still lived in North Philadelphia —we didn't move here although they owned a bakery. Business was pretty good at the time. At the bakery, we have somehow geared towards more Vietnamese customers, for some reason. Probably because we make a lot of wedding cakes.

Some of my relatives might speak Vietnamese—some might, you know, it depends on their preference and how they want to raise their kids. They'll raise them as Chinese, some according to who they marry. You know, if they married a Chinese person, Chinese. My uncles married Laotian and other races and they just raise their kids accordingly. We have a lot of languages at home: Chinese, Vietnamese, English. Our English is pretty much equal, but my sister speaks a lot of Chinese because she was raised Chinese. She doesn't speak Vietnamese, however she does understand it because people talk it. And me, well, my brother could probably speak better Vietnamese than I can, but I can speak a little of both.

The kids have Americanized, but my parents pretty much have not. They don't do anything really Americanized. They just do their usual things, traditional way. My dad, you know, got all these lanterns in the house. The whole house is pretty much traditional, I would say. Everything has to be good feng shui. They don't watch American movies. My dad will just watch the news. My parents would probably call themselves Chinese from Vietnam. But me personally, my brother, and my sister would agree that we're Americans. We're definitely Philadelphians, we're very patriotic to our sports teams. And we're Chinese Americans.

I think pharmacy's a good field—it's opportunity, an important job. You're helping patients. Some patients don't know what they're doing with medications. I'd like to educate people more about their lives, their health. Chinese herbals are a much more conservative approach and they work for many people.[2] It's a lot more conservative, it's a lot safer, and it's been around a lot longer, and it's not out there to make as much money as these pharmaceutical companies, billion-dollar companies. I'm all for it, I'm just not in the business.

For me, Chinatown has always been a home. I find myself really comfortable here. There's a lot of characteristics that wouldn't make it a home—the noise, the loitering, the traffic, the trash, the congestion. But I always like it because I feel that it's a great place to live, the center of everything. There's always people stopping by to visit me, it's never out of their way.

I have two children. One is six years old and is in kindergarten. The other is only fifteen days old. Our children are unusual in that they are exposed to two cultures. In China we respect elders and place ourselves behind them. I told my son a story from ancient China about Zhang Xiaoli's plum. He had several plums at home. He kept the smallest plum for himself, but gave the larger plums to his brothers and sisters. So I tell my son this story, using this plum as an example of Chinese tradition. I don't want him to grow up only understanding American culture. I want him to respect and love his relatives, call them more than once a year.

KeKe Wang

Born October 9, 1960 in Liuzhou, Guangxi Province, China.
Keke Wang owns and works at Asia America Travel Group in Chinatown.

I was born in Liuzhou, which is a medium-size city among Chinese cities, an industrial-based city in Guangxi province. The city has gone through great changes since I grew up there. In the downtown, you see more highrises. When I was there, there were only two bridges. Now there are six.

I had a very good English teacher. He graduated from a foreign languages college so he was very encouraging. Chinese society was beginning to open up at the end of the 1970s. Years ago, it was Russia which was popular in China.[1] But English then was beginning to replace Russian. Because of the influence of my English teacher, plus the trend in society, I decided to study English. More and more tourists from the United States, Europe, and other places came to China in the late 1970s. This required a group of tour guides who understood English. I majored in English at Normal University, which

is near Guilin, a scenically beautiful city known as "the most beautiful landscape under heaven." I was a tour guide in China for an American couple. We had a good relationship. When their tour group departed from Guangzhou, they said they'd help me come to Philadelphia to study. I was so happy to hear them say that. Through their help, I came to the United States and earned my MBA at Temple University.

In 1989, I was the first one from Mainland China to start a business in Chinatown. It was followed by a printing press, run by a Mr. Lee. Then there was the New China Bookstore, followed by a number of newspaper stands. I don't speak much Cantonese because I'm not from Guangzhou. At first, I felt like I was being excluded. But the situation is different now. All organizations are willing to welcome everybody. The atmosphere in Chinatown has changed completely.

I think young Chinese are different because they're more involved in different aspects in society. So many of them have a good education, university or higher degree, like Master's or PhD. They know that democratic society is formed by getting voices from different groups and different communities. Unless you voice what you want to do, you won't get the government's attention. Young people—because of their energy, their education, because of changes in society—are more involved. Which I think is very good. I think I'm part of that younger generation, but within the Chinese community, there are differences in younger groups. There's the younger group who was born here. I'm part of a younger group coming from China, at age twenty or thirty. Each younger group may have their own agenda.

My siblings helped me greatly because I was the youngest child in the family. Growing up, I did get a lot of love and nourishment from my older sisters and older brother. At that age I never thought that I would come to America. Even later when I was learning the language and applying to come over to America, my older sisters and brothers were still in hesitation about whether it was the right step to take, whether it was the right decision to come to America. When I was growing up in Liuzhou, my family was very close. It's very important. I have a lot of caring family members who supported me when I made each step. Before taking them, some of the steps, seem very uncertain. But you have to make a decision when opportunity appears.

When I first came, the first stop was New York City. My aunt lives there, so I lived there for two weeks but I have another aunt in Philadelphia, so we came to live in Philadelphia. At the blink of an eye, already twenty-three years have passed.

I'm from Malaysia. When I was young, I started to learn Chinese, and when I came over here I started to learn English. I arrived August 1978 in the U.S. at the age of fifteen. My aunt had already immigrated and felt that the living environment here was pretty good, so she asked my dad and their brothers and sisters to come. We lived in the suburbs for ten years. When we immigrated, everyone in my family

Soo-lin Wong

Born November 21, 1961 in Raub, Pahang State, Malaysia.

Soo-lin Wong owns Lai's Hair Salon in Chinatown.

was still young. We started school, but the older ones started to find jobs. My parents used to be Chinese herbalists in Malaysia. When we got here, they changed their occupation and worked in my aunt's restaurant. They worked there for over ten years. They had no other way. When my five siblings and I graduated high school, we wanted to find jobs or learn a skill, so we moved to Chinatown.

When we just arrived, I really missed my country, classmates, and other relatives. That was when I just arrived. But about a half year later, I got used to living here, I started school, meeting new people, and felt it was easier to get accustomed. I went back to Malaysia once sixteen years later. Things have changed completely over there. It's changed so much that I don't recognize some people. Other people, older folks, have died. I can still recognize some places, but there are highways everywhere.

In the beginning, Chinatown was really small, we didn't have any clue where Chinatown was. That was eighteen years ago. There were only a few grocery stores, other stores were really small. Over these recent years, we've developed immensely. Before, we had to go to New York to do our shopping. We had to go to New York to buy groceries, roast meats. We had to go to New York to buy everything. After living here for twenty years, wow, we see that there are so many supermarkets! There are also beauty salons and stores that sell snack foods. Things are much better than before. The Chinatown today, when new immigrants arrive, it's easier.

It's only the recent five years that I expanded my business. Philly, Delaware, New Jersey, even in King of Prussia, we have customers who come from those places.[1] Here in Chinatown we have to work seven days a week. We take turns resting. Everyone has a day off each week, but the shop opens seven days a week from 9:30 a.m. to 7 p.m. A lot of times, Asians prefer other Asians to style or cut their hair because our hair texture is very different from that of Americans.

Before our store was really small. Starting with only two people, we expanded to six but we still have to keep developing. To me this place is a family business. I feel that in order to be successful, we have to participate in teamwork. That's what I believe.

My father was a very strong man. He ruled us with an iron hand, we had to be very obedient to him, and he was the one who made the decision to move to Chinatown. My mother was Caucasian and my father was Chinese. They met at a party and I call it the marriage of the century—different cultures, different languages, different backgrounds, different ages, and yet they managed to raise five kids successfully! They were married over thirty-five years until my father passed away. It was hard, I'm sure. In those days, the law was that you couldn't even get married in Pennsylvania if the couple was of two different races.[1] They had to go to Elkton, Maryland, to get married.

I was born in North Philadelphia but grew up in Chinatown and came here when I was eight years old, so I've been in Chinatown for over

Cecilia Moy Yep

Born November 7, 1929 in Philadelphia, PA.

Cecilia Moy Yep is an activist and founding member of Philadelphia Chinatown Development Corporation (PCDC), and co-founder of the Asian American Women's Coalition. She continues to live in Chinatown.

sixty-five years. I also raised my three children in the community. When I first came here, it wasn't a nice place to live. It was adjacent to Skid Row, which bordered the community's whole eastern boundary. There were a lot of what we called "flop houses" and a lot of bars. There were only a few restaurants at that time and maybe two grocery stores. My mother and father had a grocery store on 10th Street.

Having grown up in Chinatown I felt secure and safe here, so it was only natural that I wanted to live here. I lost my husband in 1963, so it was only three years later when we found out that we were going to lose the Holy Redeemer Church and School in March of 1966 because of the Vine Street Expressway.[2] I was upset because I had already suffered a great loss and now we were going to be uprooted, and I didn't have any idea of where I was going to go or what I was

going to do. The Redevelopment Authority (RDA) had already taken homes and businesses along 9th Street and displaced many people and now they were going to take the church and the school.

I organized a town meeting, the first Chinatown ever had. Basically Chinatown was a bachelor society and there were no women in the organizations at that time. The elders said, "We can't fight City Hall," because of the language barrier. "If you want to fight, you will have to do it on your own." The meeting was held around 7 p.m. on the second floor of the On Leong Association. I had gone to Joe Lowe, the president of the Chinese Benevolent Association, and asked his support in calling the Chinese Associations to attend.[3] He agreed and notified the Associations. Concerned people from the community came as well as members of the two Churches.[4] It was attended by approximately 250 people, because the Church and School were so important.

We had to advocate for twenty years to fight the Vine Street Expressway expansion and to get relocation housing for the community. I used to live on 9th and Race, and the RDA knocked down everything around me —I was the only house on the block. My house became known as the "Chinatown Alamo." I wouldn't move until they found me adequate housing to replace what I had lost. It was that determination which resulted in a comprehensive plan for three housing development projects in Chinatown that I spearheaded in the 1980s.

Since those early victories, it has been a constant struggle continuing even today. One of the factors the community is now facing is the gentrification that could happen because of the new private developments affecting Chinatown North. This works against the community in trying to keep housing affordable. Our fight for Chinatown continues. In 2000, city officials were determined that they were going to put the stadium at 12th and Vine.[5] Like many times before, a town meeting was called and held at the Church and that's where we set up committees which became known as the "Stadium Out of Chinatown Coalition." We were successful in that too.

Looking back, I often think about how great it would be if my father were here to see what we've done to Chinatown because it's so different than what it was when he and my mother were here. He really wanted us to come to Chinatown, go to Chinese school, mingle with other Chinese children. I hope he would be proud.

In China, you work so hard, no money. If you wake up six o'clock in the morning, work till twelve o'clock at night, the whole month, the most you can make is one thousand dollars Chinese money, that's only a hundred dollars U.S. money. Hundred dollars in America, we can make that in one day. That's why immigrants want to come here.

In China, we went to school, we didn't work. The whole family works here. When my parents came to Philadelphia, my mother worked in a clothing factory from 8 a.m. to 12 a.m. She worked sixteen hours a day, leaving early and coming home very late. My father was working

Shi Xing Zeng

Born October 4, 1982 in Fuzhou, Fujian Province, China.

Shi Xing (Happy) Zeng lived with his family in Chinatown until 2002. In his spare time, he volunteers to help new immigrants.

in my uncle's restaurant in Boston. My father would work there for a month, then come back to rest for four days. He would work several weeks in a row, then accumulate his days off and take the bus back to Philadelphia to be with the family.

When we first arrived, we were afraid of being tricked by people. So living in Chinatown, we believed it was safer, like being inside our home. At first living in Chinatown was very quiet. Then, after living there for a while, I felt like I was in a well. There was so much more outside to study and learn—I lived there over ten years. I know everyone there, everything, it's all very familiar, every street and small alleyway. For ten years, I heard the fire engines. A roast duck place was three houses down from my house. In Chinatown you see the fire engine right there, everyday we hear it—whoo go, whoo come back.

Even at night time, twelve o'clock, one o'clock. Everyday we come home from school or work, we got to smell the roast duck. We got used to it, you know. Smelled it for ten years.

I worked in a clothing factory. It was a summer job. Sometimes I was short of money and I didn't want to ask my parents for money. I used heat pressure to dry the clothes. You can still see the wound on my arm left by the burning of the heat pressure. I worked there for three weeks. I earned sixty-one dollars. The boss cheated me. I worked from 8 a.m. to 6 p.m., ten hours a day. I was seventeen or eighteen at the time. The other people who worked with me were old. Old grandpas and grandmas.

We have no time to see each other when we have to work. In Chinatown, I'm most impressed by the Mid-Autumn Festival.[1] It's a time when we could see each other and have fun. Before the party, we had to do many things. We made lanterns, designed clothes, donated money, and then we helped the party at night. I helped with everything. Because I know so many people in Chinatown, they always want me to do fundraising. And I play a character on stage. I would do a play about where mooncakes come from. In the play, I find a little girl and teach her where does mooncake come from, how the mooncake's like the moon, why the mooncake's sometimes so small, and then I bite the mooncake to make the "moon" smaller and I finish the whole mooncake. In the play, the little girl cries, "Ah, brother, you eat all my mooncake," and then I run away and she follows me. Everybody, everybody from Chinatown, 500, 600 people come to the festival. It's nice.

When I first arrived, I was always with Chinese in American schools so my English was bad. When I went to high school, I was the only person from Fuzhou. So I had no choice but to go and speak English. Life forced me to speak English. So I learned English in one year at that school. There are many people who just arrived who don't speak English. They need a place to live, but when they apply for electricity, water, gas, these kinds of things, they need help. They can't read the forms, they don't know where to get this done, they don't know any of this. I regularly do things in Chinatown, helping people who need help.

End Notes

Lisa Cancelliere

1 In 1939, an exiled Chinese Archbishop, the Most Reverend Paul Yu Pin, visited Philadelphia to speak to the Chinese community. The work of the Sisters of the Holy Trinity, a missionary order already in Chinatown, and the support of Cardinal Dennis Dougherty and Reverend William Kavanagh resulted in Holy Redeemer's present structures being dedicated on October 15, 1941. In 1992, lay teachers replaced the teaching nuns at the School.

2 Over 110,000 Americans of Japanese descent, primarily those living on the West Coast, were sent to internment camps during World War II with the implementation of President Franklin Delano Roosevelt's Executive Order 9066. Approximately 20,000 Japanese Americans temporarily lived in the Santa Anita Racetrack in California while awaiting removal to the camps.

3 Dynasty Court is a complex of fifty-six Section 8 rental apartments and six commercial units at Race Street between 10th and 11th Streets completed by Philadelphia Chinatown Development Corporation (PCDC) in 1983.

Jong Kai Chin

1 Hong Kong, a British protectorate, fell to the invading Japanese in World War II on December 25, 1941. British and American soldiers then faced a string of defeats as they lost various islands in the Pacific to the Japanese military at that point in the war.

2 The Cold War was the defining post-World War II clash of political, economic, and social ideologies and systems between the Union of Soviet Socialist Republics (U.S.S.R) and the United States and its allies from roughly the end of World War II until the fall of the Berlin Wall in 1990.

3 The mutual assistance benevolent associations based on family name, occupational, village, or regional ties have historically played an important role in Chinatowns in the Americas. Especially early on when the Chinese "sojourners" living in bachelor societies were marginalized in mainstream society, they provided social services and acted as economic and cultural support networks. In many cities, including Philadelphia, the associations dominated the informal political and economic structures of the community. The Gee How Oak Tin Benevolent Association covers the family names of Chin, Wu, and Yuan.

4 Father Tom is a reference to Father Thomas Betz, Assistant Pastor of Holy Redeemer Church in Chinatown, an active member of a number of Philadelphia Chinatown organizations.

Wai Lum Chin

1 Yum cha is a transliteration of the Cantonese term for dim sum, literally to have tea.

Jayson Choi

1 In the last few years, a number of condominium units have been created in Philadelphia's Chinatown, most notably by TenTen Race and Grandview Condos, former hotels located in the neighborhood. As part of a controversial larger trend in this and many other Chinatowns, the rental averages of apartments and sale prices on homes and apartments have risen, causing many Chinese residents to move away and preventing others from staying in the community.

L.D.

1 Indonesians celebrate this national holiday annually on August 17, the anniversary of the date in 1945 when nationalists proclaimed independence from 300 years of Dutch colonial rule.

2 A traditional long-sleeved blouse worn in a variety of colors and fabrics by women in Java and Bali. European-style clothing replaced the kebaya and sarung (sarong) as everyday attire in Java in the 1930s. However it is still worn for special occasions.

3 A reference to the period during and after the Asian Financial Crisis of 1997-1999, which resulted in economic collapse and social unrest and was followed by the forced resignation of Indonesia's dictatorial president, Suharto. Ethnic Chinese, often collectively targeted in times of national tension due to a perception of their dominance in business and industry, faced escalating threats of violence during this time.

4 A place containing anywhere from two to several phone booths where people pay to make domestic or international phone calls. Warung is the abbreviation for the Indonesian term, warung telpon (a warung is a café, shop, or small business). Wartels are found in both large cities and small villages and are used alike by those who own personal phones in their homes and/or cell phones and those who do not.

5 In 2000, Philadelphia Mayor John Street proposed to build a major league baseball stadium on 12th and Vine Streets. The surrounding community in Chinatown mobilized against this proposal in very vocal protests and testimonies at public hearings. A coalition of community members and activists was formed called "Stadium Out of Chinatown" (SOCC). The proposal was successfully defeated.

Joseph Eng

1 In the 1860s, Chinese immigrants were hired by the thousands to build the Central Pacific Railroad and the Union Pacific Railroad, among other railway lines, all across the western United States. Often seen as "strikebreakers," the Chinese laborers (and other Chinese immigrants) were a frequent target for physical, political, and economic violence.

2 Thomas Jefferson University Hospital is located on 11th Street, a few blocks south of Chinatown in Philadelphia.

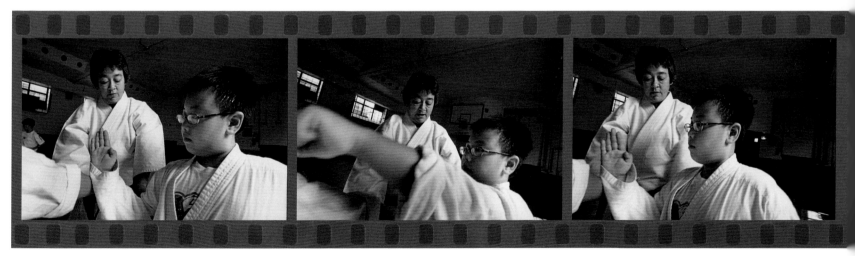

Lisa Cancelliere with Jeffrey Chau

3 The Chinese Exclusion Act passed by Congress in 1882 is the most well-known in a series of exclusionary immigration measures targeted at Asians. This Act severely limited the number and type of Chinese immigrants allowed to enter the United States. Because of the relative lack of women, the early Chinese communities in the Americas are commonly known as "bachelor societies." Restricted immigration meant that a flourishing Chinese American family life could not develop until after World War II.

4 Mao Zedong declared The People's Republic of China on October 1, 1949. The Communists had been fighting the Nationalist Party (Kuomintang, or KMT) after the Japanese surrendered in World War II.

5 China was an ally of the United States after the United States entered World War II. The Chinese Exclusion Act (see above) was repealed in 1943. The War Brides Act (1945) allowed spouses and children of U.S. military personnel to immigrate to the United States.

6 On December 7, 1941, the Japanese military bombed Pearl Harbor, an American military base in Hawaii. This event led to America's entry into World War II.

7 Returning World War II veterans could receive a college education or vocational training because of the passage of the G.I. Bill of Rights or the Servicemen's Readjustment Act (1944).

8 The Philadelphia Navy Yard, located on League Island on the Delaware River, was the first naval shipyard in the United States. Its greatest period of activity was during World War II when it employed 40,000 workers. It closed in 1995-1996.

9 Philadelphia Chinatown Development Corporation built On Lok House, a development of fifty-five Section 8 rental units for the elderly and two commercial units at 219 North 10th Street in 1984.

10 In 2000, Philadelphia Mayor John Street proposed to build a major league baseball stadium on 12th and Vine Streets. The surrounding community in Chinatown mobilized against this proposal in very vocal protests and testimonies at public hearings. A coalition of community members and activists was formed called "Stadium Out of Chinatown" (SOCC). The proposal was successfully defeated.

Joseph Eng with Jane L. Eng

Catharine Fan

1 After the Vietnam War ended, many refugees and other immigrants fled Southeast Asia from the late 1970s through the 1980s and arrived in the United States. Most refugees were from Vietnam, Cambodia, and Laos. The Southeast Asian Resource Action Center estimates about 1.3 million refugees have arrived in the United States from 1975-1998.

2 In these oral histories, people use a number of different terms to describe Fujian province and the people from Fujian ranging from Fuzhou, Fujian, Fukienese, Fujianese. To a lesser extent, interviewees also alternate between using Canton and Guangdong to describe Guangdong province. We have left the terms used by the interviewees standing.

3 The 200 block of Camac Street is a small street located on the northwest fringe of Chinatown.

4 There was some resistance in Chinatown against the building of the Philadelphia Convention Center, Pennsylvania's largest public construction project, which is located on Chinatown's western fringe. It opened in 1993 and became yet another project that cut off the growth of the neighborhood.

Bihong Guan

1 Economic policy and natural disaster in the People's Republic of China led to the "three years' difficult period" from 1959-1961. An estimated forty million people died of the famine that spread across China in that period.

2 The Great Proletarian Cultural Revolution was a campaign launched by Mao Zedong in 1966 to reinvigorate the proletarian ideals of the Communist Party. In the cultural and political chaos that followed, many died, were stripped of possessions, and/or imprisoned. Officially the Revolution ended in 1969, but many say it lasted until 1976.

3 Many thousands of student protestors overtook Tiananmen Square in Central Beijing from April to June 1989, calling for increased democracy in China. The Chinese government responded by declaring martial law. The People's Liberation Army was ordered to clear the square and on June 3rd and 4th, violence ensued. Estimates for the number of protesters killed during the incident range from 500 to 3,000. Worldwide condemnation of the massacre and ensuing human rights abuses have continued implications for U.S.-China relations. At that time, President George H.W. Bush signed a bill allowing students from China who were currently

Catharine Fan

studying at American universities and colleges to legally remain in the United States.

4 In 2000, Philadelphia Mayor John Street proposed to build a major league baseball stadium on 12th and Vine Streets. The surrounding community in Chinatown mobilized against this proposal in very vocal protests and testimonies at public hearings. A coalition of community members and activists was formed called "Stadium Out of Chinatown" (SOCC). The proposal was successfully defeated.

5 Double Ten Day (October 10, 1911) is the national day of Taiwan, the Republic of China. It commemorates the Wuchang Rebellion, which led to the collapse of the Qing Dynasty.

Wai Man Ip

1 The New Territories include 235 outlying islands that make up the largest part of Hong Kong while Hong Kong Island itself is only forty-eight miles and Kowloon, the peninsula north of Hong Kong Island, is only twenty-eight miles.

2 *Sing Tao Daily* is Hong Kong's second largest Chinese-language newspaper. It has the largest regional coverage among global Chinese communities and the second largest global coverage in the world, following the *International Herald Tribune*. *Sing Tao*, along with a number of other prominent Chinese-language papers and other media, often reflect and affect political and economic opinions of diasporic Chinese communities.

3 After the Vietnam War ended, many refugees and other immigrants fled Southeast Asia from the late 1970s through the 1980s and arrived in the United States. Most refugees were from Vietnam, Cambodia, and Laos. The Southeast Asian Resource Action Center estimates about 1.3 million refugees have arrived in the U.S. from 1975-1998.

Jayson Choi with his children Colin, Meghan, and Stephanie

Benny Lai

1 After the Vietnam War ended, many refugees and other immigrants fled Southeast Asia from the late 1970s through the 1980s and arrived in the United States. Most refugees were from Vietnam, Cambodia, and Laos. The Southeast Asian Resource Action Center estimates about 1.3 million refugees have arrived in the U.S. from 1975-1998.

2 In these oral histories, people use a number of different terms to describe Fujian province and the people from Fujian ranging from Fuzhou, Fujian, Fukienese, Fujianese. To a lesser extent, interviewees also alternate between using Canton and Guangdong to describe Guangdong province. We have left the terms used by the interviewees standing.

Eric Law

1 Thomas Jefferson University Hospital is located on 11th Street, only a few blocks south of Chinatown in Philadelphia.

2 The Philadelphia Suns is a youth community group in Chinatown that plays basketball, conducts community service, and performs lion dances at various functions.

3 Chinese Christian Church and Center is an important church and community center in Chinatown.

4 F.O.B. is slang term meaning "fresh off the boat." It is often a negative term used when referring to recent immigrants.

Chun Moy Lee

1 Mao Zedong declared The People's Republic of China on October 1, 1949. The Communists had been fighting the Nationalist Party (Kuomintang, or KMT) after the Japanese surrendered in World War II. The Chinese Communist Party aspired to follow Mao Zedong's teachings about women's rights. In the late 1950s, as the Communist party attempted to galvanize the nation's production and productivity, women were encouraged to work, especially in agriculture, as part of that larger national project.

2 Holy Redeemer Chinese Catholic Church and School is an important school and church in Chinatown.

Mitzie Mackenzie with Lena Sze

67

Romana Lee

1 Toisan or Toisanese is a term used to describe the dialect of Chinese spoken by people originally from the Toisan District of Guangdong Province, a specific area from which a very high proportion of the earliest Chinese settlers to the Americas originated.

2 PCDC is a grassroots, non-profit, community-based organization whose mission is to preserve, protect, and promote Chinatown as a viable ethnic, residential, and business community.

Wei Yew Lee

1 Bahasa Malaysia (also known as Malay) is Malaysia's official language although English, Tamil, and various dialects of Chinese are also widely spoken.

Harry Leong

1 On September 8, 1941, Chinese Christian Center opened at 1006 Race Street. In June 1942, the American Baptist Churches, the Episcopal Church, the Evangelical and Reformed Denominations, the United Methodist Church, and the Presbyterian Church united to form an inter-denominational Board of Directors. This led to the incorporation of the Chinese Christian Church and Center in July 1946, along with the purchase of the current premises for a new church building at 225 N. 10th Street.

2 General George A. McCall School is a public middle school located on 6th and Delancey Streets in Philadelphia, a few blocks south of Chinatown.

3 The first Chinese laundry in Philadelphia was founded in 1870 by a man named Lee Fong at 913 Race Street. This event is generally seen as the "beginning" of Philadelphia's Chinatown. In 1880, the first Chinese restaurant was opened above Lee Fong's laundry.

Shi Xing Zeng

4 Harry Leong makes his observations about the increasing presence of Latino workers in Chinatowns across the United States. Often from Mexico, Honduras, or El Salvador, they frequently work at Chinatown restaurants, bakeries, grocery stores, and vegetable stands.

5 Holy Redeemer Chinese Catholic Church and School is an important school and church in Chinatown.

6 The Philadelphia Suns is a youth community group in Chinatown that plays basketball, conducts community service, and performs lion dances at various functions.

7 Asian basketball leagues, particularly those of Japanese Americans and Chinese Americans, provided a social and recreational outlet for many Asian American youth from the 1920s until today.

8 Mitzie Mackenzie is the former center director at Chinese Christian Church and Center, also interviewed in our Oral History Project.

9 Toisan or Toisanese is a term used to describe the dialect of Chinese spoken by people originally from the Toisan District of Guangdong Province, a specific area from which a very high proportion of the earliest Chinese settlers to the Americas originated.

10 Jook Sing, a Cantonese term literally meaning hollow bamboo, is a negative term applied to second-generation or American-born Chinese who are Chinese in appearance but lacking Chinese culture.

11 ABC stands for American-born Chinese.

Mitzie Mackenzie

1 The American Legion, the world's largest veterans organization, has sponsored various contests and given out awards to students since its founding in 1919.

2 The first Chinese immigrants to arrive in the Americas are often referred to as "sojourners," because many of them hoped to settle back and be buried in their hometowns and villages even after living in American Chinatowns for many years.

Wei Yew Lee with Gloria Lee

3 On September 8, 1941, Chinese Christian Center opened at 1006 Race Street. In June 1942, the American Baptist Churches, the Episcopal Church, the Evangelical and Reformed Denominations, the United Methodist Church, and the Presbyterian Church united to form an inter-denominational Board of Directors. This led to the incorporation of the Chinese Christian Church and Center in July 1946, along with the purchase of the current premises for a new church building at 225 N. 10th Street.

4 This is a reference to the China Friendship Gate, which is the first authentic gate built in America by artisans from Tianjin, China (Philadelphia's sister city). This historical landmark at 10th and Arch Streets is considered one of the most visible markers of Philadelphia's Chinatown.

5 Dynasty Court (Wing Wah Yuen) is a complex of fifty-six Section 8 rental apartments and six commercial units at Race Street between 10th and 11th Streets completed by Philadelphia Chinatown Development Corporation (PCDC) in 1983.

6 Vine Street is considered the northern fringe of Chinatown. The hope of many in the community, including Philadelphia Chinatown Development Corporation (PCDC), is that Chinatown will grow into a "Chinatown North" extending from its current dimensions past Vine Street to Spring Garden, a few blocks north of Vine.

Iwan Santoso

1 The Asian Financial Crisis of the late 1990s during which Asia's economy crashed, leading to devaluation of currencies and loss of foreign investment among other effects, severely impacted Indonesia. Considerable numbers of ethnic Chinese, often collectively targeted in times of national tension due to a perception of their dominance in business and industry, left or were forced to flee Indonesia soon after the start of the economic crisis in 1997 due to escalating threats or violence against them.

2 In late 1965, then-General Suharto took control of the army and a subsequent massacre of Communists and suspected Communist Party

Iwan Santoso

sympathizers throughout Indonesia began after a coup against the current government under President Sukarno. During this time, attacks against and persecution of ethnic Chinese also ensued. This tension continued throughout 1966 when Suharto seized power from Sukarno to become Indonesia's second president and in 1967, after anti-Chinese demonstrations, Indonesia broke its diplomatic relations with China resulting in a further crackdown on Chinese-language newspapers and schools and Chinese-owned businesses.

3   There are no official census records to substantiate Santoso's estimate of the number of Indonesian immigrants in the early to mid-1990s. However, the first significant wave of Indonesian immigrants to Philadelphia arrived after 1996 due to the economic and social results of the economic crisis that swept through Asia between 1997 and 1999. Indonesian community leaders in Philadelphia currently estimate the Indonesian population to be at around an average of 5,000 people.

4   The historic Reading Terminal Market in Center City Philadelphia, one block Southwest of Chinatown, has housed vendors selling produce, meats, fish, prepared foods, and numerous other wares for over 100 years.

5   Sunday get-togethers at church is a phenomenon not applicable to all of Philadelphia's Indonesian immigrant community (e.g. Muslim Indonesians of which there is a significant population).

6   After the terrorist attacks against the United States on September 11, 2001, a slumping economy found many people without work as businesses, especially factories and warehouses, which employ numerous Indonesians and other immigrants in the Philadelphia area, saw a decrease in production quotas.

7   After September 11, 2001, the newly created Department of Homeland Security revised immigration procedures implemented by the United States' Bureau of Citizenship and Immigration Services (formerly the INS). During a period called "Special Registration," male immigrants

Chun Moy Lee with Rebecca Ng and Lena Sze

from Indonesia and other countries living or traveling to the United States were required to register themselves with local BCIS branch offices. As detention or deportation could result for those living in the United States without current legal immigration status, when faced with the new procedures, numerous individuals, both male and female, decided to return to Indonesia voluntarily.

Khai Tang

1 After the Vietnam War ended, many refugees and other immigrants fled Southeast Asia from the late 1970s through the 1980s and arrived in the United States. Most refugees were from Vietnam, Cambodia, and Laos. The Southeast Asian Resource Action Center estimates about 1.3 million refugees have arrived in the U.S. from 1975-1998.

2 "Chinese herbals" here refers to the medicinal traditions of Chinese, Japanese, Korean, Taiwanese, and Vietnamese origin, which includes use of herbs, acupuncture, breathing exercises, and other methods. This treatment is said to have been in use since the third century B.C.E.

KeKe Wang

1 Soon after its founding in 1949, Communist China sought to model many of its socialist policies on the Soviet Union's. There was regular cultural and political interchange between the two countries during this period.

Soo-lin Wong

1 King of Prussia is an outlying suburb of Philadelphia in Pennsylvania.

Cecilia Moy Yep

1 Anti-miscegenation laws were passed in thirty-nine states between 1815 and 1920. In 1967 the United States Supreme Court struck down state laws banning interracial marriage in Loving v. Virginia.

2 Philadelphia Chinatown's community activism against the threatened demolition of the Holy Redeemer Church and School for expansion of

Soo-lin Wong

the Vine Street Expressway was part of Philadelphia's "Save Chinatown Movement" (1960s to 1980s). At its height in 1973, a group of young radicals known as the "Yellow Seeds" prevented bulldozers from construction work on Vine Street under the rallying cry of "Homes, not highways."

3 The mutual assistance associations based on family name, occupational, village, or regional ties have historically played an important role in Chinatowns in the Americas. Especially early on when the Chinese "sojourners" living in bachelor societies were marginalized in mainstream society, they provided social services and acted as economic and cultural support networks. In many cities, including Philadelphia, the associations dominated the informal political and economic structures of the community.

4 The two churches referenced here are Holy Redeemer Catholic Church and School and Chinese Christian Church and Center.

5 In 2000, Philadelphia Mayor John Street proposed to build a major league baseball stadium on 12th and Vine Streets. The surrounding community in Chinatown mobilized against this proposal in very vocal protests and public hearing testimony. A coalition of community members and activists was formed called "Stadium Out of Chinatown" (SOCC). The proposal was successfully defeated.

Shi Xing Zeng

1 Organized annually since 1996 by Asian Americans United (AAU), a community social justice organization formerly located in Philadelphia's Chinatown, the Mid-Autumn Festival is a traditional lunar new year holiday celebrated in China. In these community-wide festivities, there are dance, kung fu, opera, and other performances. AAU exists so that people of Asian ancestry in Philadelphia exercise leadership to build their communities and unite to challenge oppression.

Books & Articles

Anderson, Kay J. *Vancouver's Chinatown: Racial Discourse in Canada, 1875-1980*. Montreal: McGill-Queen's University Press, 1991.

Baum, Willa K. *Transcribing and Editing Oral History*. Nashville: American Association for State and Local History, 1977.

Brown, Cynthia Stokes. *Like It Was: A Complete Guide to Writing Oral History*. New York: Teachers & Writers Collaborative, 1988.

Chew, Ron, ed. *Reflections of Seattle's Chinese Americans: The First 100 Years*. Seattle: University of Washington Press, 1994.

Resources

Grele, Ronald J. "Movement Without Aim: Methodological and Theoretical Problems in Oral History." In *Envelopes of Sound: The Art of Oral History*. Westport, CT: Praeger, 1991.

Kwong, Peter. *The New Chinatown*. New York: Farrar, Straus and Giroux, 1987.

Lee, Joann Faung Jean. *Asian Americans: Oral Histories of First to Fourth Generation Americans from China, the Philippines, Japan, India, the Pacific Islands, Vietnam and Cambodia*. New York: The New Press, 1991.

Lowe, Lisa. *Immigrant Acts: On Asian American Cultural Politics*. Durham: Duke University Press, 1996.

Nee, Victor G. and Brett de Bary. *Longtime Californ'*. New York: Random House, 1972.

Odo, Franklin, Tachiki, Amy, Wong, Buck and Eddie Wong, eds. *Roots:*

An Asian American Reader. Los Angeles: UCLA Asian American Studies Center, 1971.

Portelli, Alessandro. "Oral History as Genre." In *The Battle of Valle Giulia: Oral History and the Art of Dialogue*. Madison: University of Wisconsin Press, 1997.

Spence, Jonathan D. *The Search for Modern China*. New York: W.W. Norton & Company, 1990.

Takaki, Ronald. *Strangers from a Different Shore: A History of Asian Americans*. Boston: Little, Brown and Company 1989.

Tchen, John Kuo Wei. *New York before Chinatown: Orientialism and the Shaping of American Culture, 1776-1882*. Baltimore: Johns Hopkins University Press, 1999.

Websites

About Philadelphia's Chinatown:
  Asian Americans United: www.aaunited.org
  Asian Arts Initiative: www.asianartsinitiative.org
  Philadelphia Chinatown Development Corporation:
    www.chinatown-pcdc.com
  Philadelphia Chinatown Official Commerical Website:
    www.phillychinatown.com
  Philadelphia Inquirer Feature on Chinatown:
    www.philly.com/mld/philly/news/7929700
  Balch Institute for Ethnic Studies On-line Philadelphia Chinatown
    Exhibition: www2.hsp.org/exhibits/Balch%20exhibits/chinatown/
    chinatown.html

About Chinese American History:
  Chinese American Museum (in Los Angeles): www.camla.org
  Museum of Chinese in the Americas (in New York City):
    www.moca-nyc.org
  Organization of Chinese Americans: www.ocanatl.org
  Wing Luke Museum (in Seattle): www.wingluke.org

Rodney Atienza is a photographer committed to photojournalism for social justice. After graduating with a degree in history from James Madison University in Virginia, he worked at Project HOME, a non-profit organization combating the cycle of poverty and homelessness. There he met photographer Harvey Finkle and decided to dedicate his life to photographing social issues.

His body of work includes several series of social justice movements such as homelessness and mental health, poverty, disability rights, and advocacy for nursing home residents and inner city youth. Professional exhibitions include the solo exhibit "Footstompers: A Photographic Essay on a North Philadelphia Youth Drill Team" at Project HOME (1997) and inclusion in the group exhibit "Disabled Awareness Day" at the Equal Employment Opportunity Center (2002). His photographs have been printed in a number of publications. Most recently, his work was featured in the book *No Restraints: An Anthology of Disability Culture in Philadelphia* (edited by Gil Ott, 2002). Rodney's most current work has focused on documentation of Asian Americans in Philadelphia including Philadelphia Chinatown's struggle against the proposed building of a baseball stadium in its neighborhood in 2000 and the interviewees of the Asian Arts Initiative's Chinatown Oral History Project.

John William Chin is the Executive Director of the Philadelphia Chinatown Development Corporation (PCDC), a nonprofit organization offering affordable housing, affordable parking, commercial development, referral services, translation services, and notices of educational, employment, and financial assistance opportunities. PCDC is the oldest Asian community development corporation in the country.

Prior to PCDC, John was an international equities trader and the director of trading operations for RRAM. John is a graduate of Drexel University, where he received a degree in business administration and management information systems. He is a native of Chinatown, Philadelphia, and attended and has been a longtime volunteer with the Holy Redeemer Chinese Catholic Church and School. He serves on the board of several nonprofit organizations, and is a member of National Coalition of Asian Pacific American Community Development.

Lena Sze is a writer and activist from New York's Chinatown. Currently pursuing her Master's in Fine Arts degree at Brooklyn College, she graduated from Swarthmore College in classics and English literature. Having gained exposure to Asian American and Chinese diasporic histories through volunteering at the Museum of Chinese in the Americas and at Swarthmore College, she worked on staff at the Asian Arts Initiative from 2001 to 2003.

She has co-coordinated a number of activist and cultural organizations, including the Tri-College Chinatown Tutorial in Philadelphia's Chinatown, a college economic justice group, and a diversity organization as well as edited the campus literary magazine and progressive newspaper. Lena has won a number of literary awards and been published in *A. Magazine*, *APA Journal*, *The NuyorAsian Anthology of Asian American Writings on New York City*, and other publications. She lives in Manhattan's Chinatown.

Contributors

John Kuo Wei (Jack) Tchen is a historian and cultural activist. Since 1975, he has been studying interethnic and interracial relations of Asians and Americans and helping to build cultural organizations. Jack is the founding director of the A/P/A (Asian/Pacific/American) Studies Program and Institute at New York University and an Associate Professor of the Gallatin School for Individualized Study and the History Department of the Faculty of Arts and Sciences. In 1980, he co-founded the New York Chinatown History Project, which was later renamed the Museum of Chinese in the Americas, in New York City. Jack has consulted for a number of museums and associations and served on the boards of many historical and cultural organizations.

His most recent book is the award-winning *New York Before Chinatown: Orientalism and the Shaping of American Culture, 1776-1882* (Johns Hopkins University Press, 1999). He has also authored *Genthe's Photographs of San Francisco's Old Chinatown* (1984), which won an American Book Award, and edited and introduced Paul C. P. Siu's classic study *The Chinese Laundryman: A Study of Social Isolation* (1987).

Acknowledgements

This publication and the Asian Arts Initiative's Philadelphia Chinatown Oral History Project would not have been possible without the people who grew and nurtured it from a fledgling idea to the reality of a community project it became. We thank and acknowledge the participants listed below, many of whom played multiple roles.

Interviewees/Narrators
Lisa Cancelliere, Jong Kai Chin, Wai Lum Chin, Jayson Choi, L.D., Joseph Eng, Catherine Fan, Bihong Guan, Wai Man Ip, Benny Lai, Eric Law, Chun Moy Lee (Chut Po), Romana Lee, Wei Yew (Leslie) Lee, Harry Leong, Mitzie MacKenzie, Linda Ng, Iwan Santoso, Khai Tang, Helen Wang, KeKe Wang, Soo-lin Wong, Cecilia Moy Yep, Shi Xing (Happy) Zeng

Additional Participants in Interviews
Janne Chin (with Wai Lum Chin), Mei Hing (Linda) Leung (with Lisa Cancelliere)

Featured in Photo Portraits
Jane L. Eng (with Joseph Eng), Hoy Mant Moy (with Cecilia Moy Yep)

Interviewers
Gloria Chan, Liz Cho, Helen Faller, Roko Kawai, Kelly Lau, Michelle Lo, Aryani Manring, Dahlia Setiyawan, Rana Sindhikara, John Smagula, Lena Sze, Linda Tsui, Tanya Wansom, Yoonmee Chang and her Asian American Ethnic Enclaves in Literature class at University of Pennsylvania (Spring 2002): Lauren Buckalew, Christine Choi, Jane Choi, Olivia Hayden-Yee, Henry Huang, Quyen Le, Nick Tang

Translation/Transcription
Teena Bounpraseuth, Eric Chen, Wendy Cheung, Uyen Doan, Liming Guan, Qiuting (Christina) He, Gena Heng, Steve Huang, Rena Kha, Rebecca Ng, Chon Phoeuk, Mary Seng, Jacqueline Wong, Melody Wong, Yun Zeng, Michael Zhao, Magnum Translation Company

Chinatown Contacts & Organizations
Father Yulianus Astanto Adi, Father Thomas Betz, John Chin, Chinese Christian Church and Center, Lai Har Cheung, Holy Redeemer Chinese Catholic Church and School, Kurt Jung, Tim Lee, Romana Lee, Linda Leung, George Moy, Philadelphia Chinatown Development Corporation (PCDC), Gerard Pescatore, Andy Toy, Carol Wong, Jackie Wong

Additional Assistance
Edward Carlson, Joseph Gonzales, Qiang Huang, Debora Kodish, Cynthia Lee, Dharma Naik, Ajay Nair, Nadine Patterson, Dmae Roberts, Steve Rowland, Angela Reyes, Gary San Angel, Juliet Shen, Sean Stoops, Karen Su, John Kuo Wei Tchen, Kathy Uno

Special thanks to Wendy Lee and Kathryn Wilson

Additional thanks to the following organizations and individuals for providing financial support for our Chinatown Oral History Project and the publication of *Chinatown Live(s)*.

Major Funders ($5,000+)
New City Community Press
Pennsylvania Historical and Museum Commission
Samuel S. Fels Fund

Sponsors ($1,000+)
Linda Lee Alter
C. J. Huang Foundation
PNC Bank
Vietnam Restaurant

Supporters ($500+)
Asian Bank
Choi Funeral Home
Greater Philadelphia Tourism Marketing Corporation
Hazel Isa
University of the Arts

Friends ($100+)
Asian Student Association of the University of the Sciences in Philadelphia
Sue Ishikawa
Mytili Jagannathan
Madelyn and James Kawano
Marcia and Edward Kung
Sophia Lee and Michael O'Halloran
Evan and Hao-Li Tai Loh
Patricia Ma
Mitzie Mackenzie
Multicultural Affairs Congress/PCVB
Jena Osman
Philadelphia Chinatown Development Corporation
Andy and Pat Toy

Asian Arts Initiative

www.asianartsinitiative.org

The Asian Arts Initiative is grounded in the belief that the arts
can provide an important political and cultural voice for the Asian
American communities in Philadelphia. We are a community arts
center where artists and everyday people explore and express
our diverse experiences as Asian Americans.

New City Community Press

www.newcitypress.org

New City Community Press is grounded in the belief that
writing is an implicit organizing tool that can produce
social change. We imagine writing as an act that can project
us beyond the parameters of individual selfhood into the
body politic. To that end, New City works with communities
struggling to gain cultural and political representation,
aiding them in recording and distributing their stories to
the larger public. We believe that through the inclusion of
these voices into daily life, alternative ways of speaking,
writing, and communicating manifest themselves, ultimately
re-envisioning the promise of community.

Publisher: Steve Parks, Syracuse University
Outreach Coordinator: Nicole Meyenberg

Publications:

Chinatown Live(s): Oral Histories from Philadelphia's Chinatown

*Espejos y Ventanas/Mirrors and Windows: Oral Histories of Mexican
Farmworkers and Their Families*

No Restraints: An Anthology of Disability Culture in Philadelphia

Nourish Your Soul: A Community Cookbook

Open City: A Journal of Community Arts and Culture (Vols. 1 and 2)

*The Forgotten Bottom Remembered: Stories from a Philadelphia
Neighborhood*

Chinatown Live(s) Staff

Editor
Lena Sze

Photographer
Rodney Atienza

Oral History Project Coordinators
Roko Kawai, 2004
Lena Sze, 2002-2003

Project Director
Gayle Isa, Executive Director, Asian Arts Initiative

Distributor
New City Community Press

Design
The Market Street Group

Printed in Iceland by Oddi Printing.